What Just Happened?

Living the Redeemed Life
(When All Hell Breaks Loose)

Tracy Graves Stevens

What Just Happened?

Living the Redeemed Life

When All Hell Breaks Loose

© 2017

VoicePenPurpose™ Publishing

Cover Design by Eddie Egesi

All rights reserved.

No part of this book may be reproduced in any form without permission in writing from the author. Reviewers may quote brief passages in reviews.

Published 2017

ISBN 978-0-9978394-8-7

DISCLAIMER

No part of this publication may be reproduced or transmitted in any form or by any means, mechanical or electronic, including photocopying or recording, or by any information storage and retrieval system, or transmitted by email without permission in writing from the author.

Dedication

For all those who almost gave up hope when life introduced a *revision* that required faith's *vision*

Table of Contents

Preface...........pg. i

Introduction The Event...........pg. vii

1 Detour Ahead...........pg. 1

2 A Crisis of Faith – Or Is It? ....pg. 25

3 Really God? Digging Ditches in the Valley...........pg. 50

4 Empty...........pg. 69

5 Empty...Continued...........pg. 88

6 Just God and Me (Heaven is Looking Pretty Good Right Now)...........pg. 102

7 Is That a Light? ....pg. 129

8 Knowing Your Identity – You are Reclaimed! ....pg. 147

9 God Loves the Overcomer – You are Restored! ....pg. 168

10 You are Rejoiced! ....pg. 187

Afterword ....pg. 207

Preface

What just happened?

My life was moving on its regular, predictable path and suddenly it was shifted from a smooth, paved highway to a bumpy off-road. The visible things of life had been redefined, resulting in an invisible inside of me that almost shattered my future – and my faith.

One thing we are guaranteed in life is that nothing is guaranteed. When the *stuff* of life happens we scurry to find safety - but what do you do when the safety net is not readily available or it seems as if God is silent? Have you ever tried to save yourself? When your spouse is walking out the door after many years of marriage – how do you save yourself? When you've just received a diagnosis that the pain you were feeling is not a strained muscle, but cancer– how do you save yourself?

We all will experience moments where it literally feels as if we are time-warped out of our normal life existence into a place that is unknown and unwanted. In this book, you will journey with me through two redefining moments in my life. Redefining because I did not realize how much I relied on their existence for my identity until they were gone. God has a way of allowing life excursions. These excursions you might never choose for yourself – well, maybe we sometimes choose them through our choices or actions, but many times we are the unwitting recipients of circumstances and even other people's decisions. Sometimes, the unplanned shifts can be easy to adjust to - but those tough ones – they can make you wonder if God really loves you or hears your cries for help at all.

My testimony describes how I fell victim to my fears while listening to the wrong 'inner voice' when my life veered off its familiar course. I have always been fascinated by the stories in the Bible where the protagonist overcomes the situation they are facing. What happens when you become the protagonist in your own difficult story? It is easier to read about than to experience – that is for sure.

Though I could proclaim my faith to anyone who asked (or didn't), my ability to really trust God was tested to degrees that pulled from every area of my life. It was during this particular season that I let fear interfere (or 'enter-fear') with my life which left me 'dis-couraged' (in other words I lost my courage). This book lays out the lessons I learned to truly understand what the Bible says about our identity in Jesus Christ and, more importantly, His tremendous love for each one of us. Most of us know that God is a loving God. We are taught this from a very young age in learning the song *Jesus Loves Me*. But if we know it, why is it so hard to respond confidently when the tough things of life come flying our way? I share my testimony because I learned that unplanned 'life excursions' can be lonely. They can feel desolate and can drain you of every cycle of energy and hope you ever had - and I don't want you to feel alone.

I wrote this book because, as a longtime believer in Christ, I was also forced to admit that I had reached a place in my faith journey where I had become a little too comfortable. I had become relaxed in my relationship with God and in my expectations of how He should respond to the needs of my life. Nothing is necessarily wrong with that, but remember – faith is a verb. You must keep moving in your faith. As you read, you will see how God had to jar me out of my comfort zone, to get my attention, and get me back on purpose. I have a tremendous faith in the Lord, but you never know the level of your faith until it is challenged and that is where, as my mother used to say, *the rubber meets the road.*

Our testimonies are meant to offer personal stories to attest to God's movement in our lives and His love for us. When we share how God works in the challenging times of life, it girds us up and keeps the enemy at bay. It reminds us- we are in this together.

This book describes the promises of Isaiah 43:1-2 and the dependence the Bible speaks to when it says we can rely on God in troubled times because we are redeemed. We are redeemed and God is the Redeemer – and He loves to meet us right where we are - no matter where we are on life's spectrum.

I also use the story of Joseph in Genesis 39-50 as a basis to demonstrate God's restoring power and presence as we go through life. We are reminded with Joseph, that we are not alone when life takes an unexpected and painful detour. The prayers presented at the opening of each chapter are my interpretation of what I think Joseph would have prayed to God as he was going through his various trials in life and imprisonment.

As you read, keep in mind that some events in our lives, no matter how painful, can offer the best opportunities to grow our faith. Though I have the benefit of the passage of time and prayer to see the outcome of my story – it was not easy to endure at the time. I had to realize, and I hope you do too, that you really can get up when the bottom falls out of life.

The roles we play, or the relationships we are in, are not our identities – our identity is in Jesus Christ. Surviving life's changes will be much easier when we can see ourselves through the loving eyes of our Lord and Savior. My hope is this book will lay out a strategy for you to overcome the pitfalls life offers (prayerfully before they come) and allow you to see that you *can* not only get up but also thrive by hearing what God says and holding onto it. It may not be easy, but it will be all worth it in the end.

> *Behold, I will do a new thing,*
> *Now it shall spring forth;*
> *Shall you not know it?*
> *I will even make a road in the wilderness*
> *And rivers in the desert.*
> *Isaiah 43:19*

> *Jesus Christ is the same yesterday, today, and forever.*
> *Hebrews 13:8*

Introduction

Dear God –

I am not really sure what just happened. I was happily fulfilling my duties for my master, Potiphar, and his wife came in and started to flirt with me. She has done this before, but this time she was more aggressive. As I ran out of the house to avoid her, she grabbed my cloak and it slipped off of me. She showed Potiphar the cloak when he returned home and told him I tried to lie with her.

I have done everything my master has asked of me and he has been blessed because you have blessed me. I don't understand why he wouldn't even listen to me or believe that I would do anything to disrespect him or his marriage. Now I sit in prison, not sure what will happen next.

Love, Joseph

The Event

"I'm sorry, Tracy, but the Board has decided to go in another direction."

Those words hung in the air like the dust particles you see floating through the sunlight shining into a room. They just hang there, real, but you don't think of them as part of the air you breathe.

I remember thinking, what does that mean, *We have decided to go into another direction?* What direction would that be? And was this the decision of the entire Board? There is no 'we' here, just you, one person sitting across from me in a room with the door closed.

Heck, I just stepped out of the office for a moment and came back to you talking about...*another direction*. I almost felt I heard an echo with these words as if I were speaking into a sea shell – *another direction, 'rection, 'rection, 'rection...*

I should have had a clue when I came back to the conference room I had been working in and could not log onto my laptop. I remember thinking, "Am I that fat-fingered that I can't type my password in correctly three times in a row? Oh well, I guess I'd better call the IT folks to find out what is up with my computer."

...another direction. This new direction was a defining point in my life; the brakes had been hit or maybe it was a crash because the brakes gave out. I tried to be stoic because that is what we are taught in business. Never let them see you cry, especially if you are a woman. Though I had violated this unspoken rule many a time during a company celebration, an employee sickness, or emotional acknowledgments, this was different. Previously, I never did the ugly cry, maybe just a little sniffle, but today – out came the tears. It became that uncontrollable kind of cry where you feel the hiccups coming on. "Please, God – don't let me completely lose it – not now. They cannot see me so upset, not like this."

At this point, the messenger of this life-changing "news" left the room. I began to think of the days leading up to this moment – certain members of my staff whispering and suddenly ending their conversations when I came around. Closed-door conversations in a culture where I cherished open doors. I found out later, this termination was much more than just a decision to go into another direction. Other colleagues who had been close to me had another prevailing agenda which included purchasing the company... without me. I was devastated.

As I packed up my things, everything that I had experienced in recent years flashed before my eyes. The grief of losing my in-laws and my father over the past three years and it's almost demolishing impact on my marriage. The thought of how I would care for my own ailing mother whose medical care and related expenses were mounting as each year passed – and now being faced with the elimination of the income I relied on to care for her. I could remember some days in the past few years when the stress of trying to keep the company on track was a welcome relief to what was going on at home. I even thought about the milestones we celebrated during my tenure in this job in this very conference room I was standing in. Strategy sessions, board meetings, interviews, proposal development, partner dialogues - we were overcomers in a tough market. This was until recent events, as the industry standards began to change requiring more and more financial investment to keep up.

I know, I thought, I will call my husband Garry. He always has a calming effect on me. He will talk me through this. As I started to dial his number my hands were shaking and, for a moment, I could not remember what number to dial. Thank God for speed dial. Wait, what number did I just call? I felt so disoriented. I reasoned that he rarely answers his mobile phone at work – that damn cell phone reception! I tried to convince myself not to cry.

He answered, "Hey, honey!"

I immediately broke out into a whine/yelp that I could not stop.

"Garry, I think I am getting fired."

I was so confused I could not even say it with finality.

After being surprised by what I had said, he went silent for a few seconds. Then he responded in that affirmative way I have come to love in him, "Walk out with your head high, honey."

At this point I, like Joseph in the Bible, looked up to God and asked, "What just happened?"

Detour Ahead

Chapter 1

Dear God –

It has been a couple of days now and Potiphar has still not come to get me out of this prison. Surely, he knows my character and believes I would never do something like what I am accused of. Why won't his wife admit that she was the one who tried to sleep with me? I am confused now. Is this the end of my career? My life? This is not new as I have been at a low point before when my brothers buried me in that pit but somehow this feels different. I am trusting you will come to save me again, God – right? Are you there?

Love, Joseph

Life happens. This is one of those phrases we hear all of the time about living. As we grow up we are told life is full of adventures and change. In the movie *Forrest Gump*, Forrest Gump's mother (played by Sally Field) told a young Forrest, "life is like a box of chocolates. You never know what you're gonna to get." I don't know about you, but when I get one of those big boxes of chocolates I never really eat all of them. I just look for the ones I may like that have nuts or caramel inside. In general, I really don't like to be surprised with something that I may not like – and that is how I like to live life. I expect the unknown to happen, but I prefer to have an idea of what is going to happen next. I want to *know what I know* per se. For example, I want to know my route and what is waiting for me at the end of the drive. Seem boring? Not to me! A little diversion is not bad, but it has to be an enjoyable diversion, not something that is going to take too much of my time or keep me away from the stuff I need to do. Do you live like this? If so, we could be buddies. At least buddies until it is time for me to go home and do routine things like homework with my daughter – get what I am saying?

Why is it when we are being prepared for "life happening" around us, we aren't told about the "real life" part? I think when people say "life happens" it is meant to get us ready for change, but "real life" is something totally different. "Real life" is something that changes your whole perspective on this human experience. It makes you second guess decisions you have made your entire life. "Real life" events make you change the way you look or dress. It may even make you change your address. "Real life" events can take you on a journey that has no easy path. I think of global positioning systems (GPS) that offer you the option of the shortest or the fastest routes. "Real life" takes you on that other GPS option, the one I rarely ever choose – the alternative route. Why don't I like choosing it? It should offer some adventure, right? I believe I, like many, don't choose it because we aren't really sure where it is going to take us so we stay on the safe paths. The only difference between assistance from a navigational tool and "real life" is one does not necessarily give you a choice. "Real life" events just happen and as we journey through them, there is no guarantee where they are going to lead us and quite frankly, sometimes these events kind of suck.

This is how I felt when going through *The Event*. As I mentioned earlier, I had recently experienced some significant changes prior to losing my job. For example, my mother-in-law passing away as a result of Alzheimer's was definitely "real" life. It was a journey that was not only hard to experience, it had an emotional impact that I had never seen before on my husband. Can you imagine having someone that birthed and raised you to look you in the face and not recognize you? This was a tough experience to go through - both as a child and, in my case, as a witness. Alzheimer's has a way of taking a trusted familiarity out of the relationship and it can bring forth unexpected responses from all that have a connection to the situation.

Shortly after she passed away, my husband and I had the experience of dealing with the lengthy illness and subsequent passing of both of our fathers over a short, overlapping period of time. Those two experiences were really tough and it almost caused the demise of my marriage. This was "real life," but somehow a bit more acceptable because we knew at some point we would be faced with losing our parents. It was never easy, but as they aged we started to prepare ourselves for the unwelcome inevitable.

To cope with his own life experiences my father used to say the phrase, "Everybody has a birthday and everybody dies – no big deal." Uh...okay, Dad. Minimizing these events to regular, everyday occurrences doesn't make it easier, especially when you are faced with the latter. And what about all of the other events in between? The ones you don't really see coming and they force you to have to rebuild a part of your life. A life threatening health diagnosis. A spouse heading out the door. An economic shift that kills your savings. Losing a job with bills to pay. Or, like Joseph in our opening passage, being terminated from a position and subsequently being imprisoned for something he did not do. These events go beyond normal life expectations and can be traumatizing.

What did I feel?

I have to admit, after *The Event*, the recovery process for me was a slow one. One embedded with a lot of tissues, red noses, and screaming matches at imaginary people. Okay, not really imaginary people, but I did have some loud imaginary discussions (in my head and in front of the mirror) giving You/We a piece of my mind – it helped some. And I learned, you have to allow yourself to feel what you are feeling. It takes time to get back up. Time because you first have to realize you can get up. When something is taken that is so close to what defines you (in your mind at least) you have to face the future of a new definition. The reality is, God has already defined you – you just have to see and hear what He is saying to you. Many times we define ourselves through the lens of the world and, even though He blesses us through the process, we are devastated when that definition changes in any way. That is exactly what I grappled with after *The Event* occurred. How do I define myself going forward?

What does God say?

Proverbs 3:5 says *"Trust in the LORD with all your heart and lean not on your own understanding."* When detours come in life, our first reaction is to reason with ourselves to understand what just happened.

I know I did.

I replayed every scene or event in my mind to see what I could have changed to keep me off the broken, detoured road I found myself on. My own limited understanding said, "maybe I should have fired that person or not signed the lease on that fancy office space." Though these were choices that were made to further the company, I was now questioning if they were actions that led up to my termination.

I believe the tendency to second-guess ourselves when things happen is a natural coping mechanism to lessen the pain or impact of events when they happen.

It is as if the process of reliving upsetting events over and over in our minds will change the outcome. We all tend to dwell on the things we think we could have done differently as if it would keep the unexpected thing from happening. Whatever the triggering moment was, it is now in the past. Though we may be able to impact the future, we can't change the events that have already occurred. I think that is why God gave us Proverbs 3:5 – to trust in Him and to keep us from dwelling in the land of "what if?" and get us to move to the land of, "what are the possibilities?"

Don't get me wrong, there *are* times our fingerprints are on the knife that just stabbed us in our own back. In those cases, some retrospective thinking will help to understand our behavior to keep some events from repeating themselves. These are what I call "head bumps." Head bumps are those areas where we know we probably contributed to the eventual outcome. We tend to remember things when they come suddenly and hurt – like a bump on the head. Many times, the decisions we make in life are made to delay or prohibit a potential head bump. We do this for obvious reasons; nobody likes pain! Unfortunately, sometimes those very decisions can lead up to the exact thing we are trying to avoid. For example, not ending an unhealthy relationship or avoiding obvious toxic behavior from others because you don't want to be alone.

Eventually, the breakup or hurt comes, one way or another. A head bump is acquired. Even when we try to control our head bump experiences, we can't really predict their impact on the future. When I have talked to friends going through a divorce, they wondered if they had dressed differently or if they hadn't gained weight or if they had more sex, maybe their spouse would not be leaving. Those head bumps still may not have kept the spouse from leaving. Sometimes when the reality of life happens, there is nothing we can do about it. It can be the result of a decision another person makes and we may just be the unfortunate recipient. This is why God says not to trust our own understanding of what has happened. Despite our hurt, we shouldn't try to understand every aspect the situation or spend all of our time thinking about the pain.

Another part of dealing with real life is you can get caught up in what others may be thinking about you. This was a big issue for me after I was fired. I worried so much about what people were thinking about me that it almost became disabling. For a while, I would not even try to look for another job because I was worried about my reputation. What would my old company say about me if called for a reference? I wondered if they had laughed as I packed my stuff up and headed out the door. I was really bothered by the potential questioning of my skills and, ultimately, my integrity by a future employer.

"...lean not on your own understanding"

The problem with all of this was I was not looking at the situation through the Word of God. He tells us in 2 Chronicles 20:15, "the battle is not ours it is the Lord's." The Bible also tells us that our reputation ultimately lies with the

Lord. God is the one that knows what happens in our lives and He really does not care what man thinks about His children. God is the one who determines if we get the ultimate prize which is getting into heaven (Revelations 3:5) or if we get that new job here on earth. I suspect He really would rather we focus on what He wants us to do next rather than worry about what someone else is saying. Amen! Do you think Jesus cared what people thought as He was casting the moneychangers out of the temple (Matthew 21:12-13) or healed the man with the shriveled hand on the Sabbath (Mark 3:1-6)? I know these situations don't compare to what I went through in losing a job but Jesus lived a life to set examples for us when we face "real life" challenges.

The reality is, we don't have a magic mirror to see into the future. I imagine Joseph felt the same way when he found himself imprisoned falsely – accused of trying to sexually seduce Potiphar's wife. He was handed a detour that landed him in a place of uncertainty - what would happen next? I'm sure he worried about his reputation, the questioning of his actions and his future. God knew this about Joseph and knows this about us. He knows we are hurt and are anxious about the unknown, but He does not want us to dwell in this place too long. He asks us to trust Him. Stop worrying, God will work it out for good.

"Trust in the Lord with all of your heart and lean not on your own understanding"

If we pay attention to God's direction for us in life, we will often find our ourselves in the reset position where it will require us to shift our focus from ourselves and our problems and putting it all on the Lord. Easier said than done, I might add. 1 Peter 5:7 says "Cast all of your cares upon the Lord, because He cares for you." It doesn't say *some* but *all* of your cares upon Him. The majority of the Bible is about trusting God through everything life has to offer and the amazing thing is God really, really wants us to give our stuff to Him. No matter how messy, or sad, or guilty or confusing, He wants us to give it to Him even if it is a yucky pile of multiple things going on. God still says, "pile it on." He can handle it. Genesis 18:14a says:

"Is anything too hard for the LORD?"

God wants our trust, but not what I call a 'head trust' or the mind/intellectual part of us that is constantly reasoning. Instead, He wants the 'heart trust' that goes all in and brings the rest of us with it. If you have ever been in love, you know what I mean – when your heart falls in love, it takes everything with it including your mind. I guess that is why we sometimes can't think straight in the early stages of a relationship. Funny thing is, God was even thinking about this for us when we enter into relationships with others and warned us in Proverbs 4:23 to guard our hearts because the issues of life come when it is not protected appropriately.

When I think of love, I tell my daughter all of the time that the mind is the referee for the heart and the other physical parts of our bodies (e.g. lust/passion/senses). There are times the mind screams at us "No, don't do that! - Run!"

God is asking us in Proverbs 3:5 to do the *opposite* when it comes to Him. To not listen to our mind, but to go all in and to trust Him with our heart, our fears, our emotions, our dreams – our future. His direction belies our logic. Trusting God requires us to be able to hear *His* guidance for us. In order to do this you must be in a relationship with Him to make sure you can distinguish *His* voice from your own. I believe the voice of God is something that comes from deep within. It is something I liken to how I can recognize the voice of my daughter in a crowd – when I hear it I know it because I spend so much time with her and I am her mother. God is our Father and He knows the voice of His sheep (John 10:27). You are His sheep and He is always looking out for you to guide you.

Learning to trust in God is what is needed if you find yourself in a reset status. We need to reset our focus on our Savior. He will help us to begin the recovery process. Just like the GPS systems in our cars, God will 'recalculate' our path when a detour comes. We just have to be willing to let

God guide us even if it takes us through the alternate, complicated and possibly unexpected route.

"In all your ways submit to him, and he will make your paths straight." Proverbs 3:6

Submitting to God seems like it should easy enough, so why is it difficult in reality? Could it be that it is related to that other word that sometimes makes us uneasy especially when it comes to relationships – submission? The word *submission* implies that we are giving up a piece of ourselves for someone else to control. It is perceived as some kind of power imbalance where, if we submit, we will enslave ourselves in some way. I sometimes believe it is the one impediment to making good marriages *great* marriages. Or even blocking what we think is a good relationship with God from becoming a *great* relationship with God. Why? Because there is a natural tendency to think we are entitled to control certain or all aspects of our lives. We think we should be able to pick and choose what we want to submit and it should all work out in the end. And yes, God does give us that freedom to choose.

Unfortunately, full submission isn't a "little bit here or a little there" proposition because it involves giving up a core piece of ourselves – our trust. When we submit in our jobs, we go in with the expectation that if we do a dictated task we will get paid. There is a level of trust in this equation. When it comes to relationships, we are hurt if someone does not respond in the way we expect or betrays the more personal elements of our being. True submission means going deeper into the power we release to others. By not submitting we may be trying to protect ourselves or our territory. Believe me, I am still a neophyte in this submission game especially when it involves person-to-person submission. Admittedly, after I lost my job, my always-optimistic expectation of people turned to caution. I learned that sometimes it is good to hold back, especially if the person I am submitting to is using their relational power to hurt me and not benefit me. You would not want to submit yourself fully to someone who is not necessarily seeking sound wisdom to guide their lives, right? See Proverbs 4:23 again. But when I think on this further, how on earth could I know what was in another person's heart?

That is where Proverbs 3:6 comes in. Merriam Webster defines submission as "the state of being obedient: the act of accepting the authority or control of someone else." When you think of this in relation to God, submitting to Him means giving God full authority over our lives. It means being obedient. The Bible says, "obedience is better than sacrifice" (1 Samuel 15:22). In giving God authority over our lives, we are able to release the worry of wondering what will happen next; of what others motives may be or would have been. No second-guessing. No worrying. He is mapping this thing out for us because He knows us.

God wants us to give him our pain and poverty.

God knows us better than we do because He created us and He knows our response to the disappointments in life.

God also knows that Satan knows our weaknesses too and will try to leverage our pain, frustrations, and disappointments into a response that will not only distract us but has the potential to destroy us. 1 Peter 5:8 says Satan's number one goal is to seek, kill and do away with our faith and ultimately our sense of what it means to live happily. He tries to get our attention in many ways – through temptation, through other people and through our response to the emotional pains of living life. Satan knows we will experience loss and hurt and I think one of the doors we open to his destruction is when we try to heal and medicate our pain by ourselves.

When unpleasant events happen, the enemy starts working immediately in our heads as we try to process our feelings. He says, "let's go shopping" or "let's have a drink" to dull the impact of our wounds. We start seeking ways to fix our situation and to make ourselves feel better. We may lash out at others. We get angry. We may even try to rectify our situations by doing some kind of harm or vengeful act to get back at what the offending person/situation has done to us. I know my imaginary conversations mentioned earlier may have included an imaginary fist hitting the imaginary person's face. Though there was no possibility of me doing this in real life, those were the thoughts in my mind at the time. I know that these responses may feel good for a minute, but they have no long-term impact. What has happened to you has still happened and you still have to deal with your feelings and figure out your next move.

In Proverbs 3:5, God's promise to us in return for our submission is *He will make our paths straight*. What a promise! God has volunteered to be the pilot of our lives and wants to take control of this detour that has introduced itself into our journey. He is doing it willingly and has stated that He is a safe place for us so we don't have to worry about the power imbalance of submission (Matthew 11:29). We can trust Him with our submission because He has our best interests at heart. This means I don't have to worry about what other people are going to do to me or figure out what they are thinking – He is going to do this for me. As we journey through Joseph's story we will see how God not only restores him, but uses Joseph's experiences for good; to glorify God Himself. He will take this pain and hold it and love it and make it work for good. We may not see it now, and I didn't at the time, but God sees it and knows how to transform our pain into something glorious. So, let's get started doing some *submitting*.

Redeemed Reflections

First Steps When the Bottom Falls Out of Life:

- Be still and give it to God.

- Trust in God – Listen to Him, He will direct you during this time.

- Stop and listen. Develop your 'spiritual ear' for listening to God.

- Don't criticize or second guess yourself – your logic is not logical during times of extreme change and stress.

  Remember, God is your safe place. Pray and seek His counsel and care.

Postscript to Chapter 1:

You can only experience the joy and fellowship of God that I am speaking of if you are in a relationship with Him. If you have not accepted the life-giving offer of his Son Jesus Christ, as your Savior, now is the time.

One thing I have learned, especially as a result of these events, is that life can change in an instant. It is always good to be prepared for what is to come and to know that God sees our life in its entirety – not just specific events we go through. I am so glad I knew the Lord when *The Event* occurred. God's love surely carried me through those tough moments. The Bible says in Joel 2:32:

And it shall come to pass, that whoever calls on the name of the Lord shall be saved. For in Mount Zion and in Jerusalem there shall be deliverance, as the Lord has said, among the remnant whom the Lord calls.

This verse is important because we sometimes think that God will not hear or help us because of things we have done in life. That maybe what we are going through is because we are in a state of perpetual punishment and God could never love us because of our past (or present). This thinking goes totally against God's definition and offering of grace and, as Joel 2:32 states, God's grace is available to everyone - not some - but everyone. No matter where you are in life. No matter what you have done. That is why Jesus Christ died on the cross for our sins - to give us new life and a hope. If you don't know Jesus, the next step is simple. Pray the following prayer and Jesus will take care of the rest:

"Jesus, I know that I am a sinner and need a Savior. I am truly sorry I have broken your laws and I want to turn away from my past sinful life. Please forgive me. I believe that You are the Son of God and died for my sins on the cross and rose again. I invite You, Jesus Christ, to become the Lord of my life, to rule and reign in my heart from this day forward. I receive you as my Lord and Savior. In Jesus' name, I pray. Amen."

If you prayed this prayer from your heart, congratulations – You are a child of the living and loving God,

Jesus Christ! Angels are celebrating right now! You are covered by the blood of Jesus for *the events* and any challenge that may lie ahead for you. To grow closer to Him, the Bible tells us to follow up on our commitment. The following steps will help you:

- Find a local church where you can worship God with other believers.
- Get <u>baptized</u> as commanded by Jesus Christ.
- Tell someone else about your new faith in Christ.
- Get a Bible and spend time with God each day. It does not have to be a long period of time. Just develop the daily habit of praying and reading His Word. Ask God to increase your faith and your understanding of the Bible.
- Seek fellowship with other followers of Jesus. Find a group of believing friends to answer your questions and support you.

A Crisis of Faith – Or Is It?"

Chapter 2

Dear God –

It's me again, Joseph. I have been praying and trying to keep my head up but it is getting harder and harder to do. I can't believe I am still in prison. Surely Potiphar knows by now that these charges against me are not true. It has been a while since I was cast into this place and even though the warden has been kind to me, this is not where I should be. Is there anything You can do to get me out of here?

Love, Joseph

For the 72 hours following *The Event,* I truly felt like I had a hole in my heart. My entire spirit was heavy and a feeling I can only describe as emptiness overwhelmed every cell of my body. Like a soap opera actor, I would break out into tears instantly, sometimes for no apparent reason. I was always a person who thrived on my daily routine and it would stress me out if anything took me away from that routine. Now I was struggling - what is my routine now? Taking my daughter, Madison, to school was a part of my 'before' tasks, but these past few days of driving up to the school in my yoga pants while everyone was dressed in their work clothes was making me a bit crazy. I had to admit (to myself and to God) - I hate this!

There is a reason I am not an actor. I'm terrible at it! Trying to smile at the other parents, especially the ones I always spoke to, when I was on the verge of tears was hard; very hard.

They would ask, "How is it going?" and I had to answer, trying to hide my insincerity, "Blessed, how about you?"

It was all I could do to get back into my car to drive to the safe but vast emptiness of my home. My home life had not changed. But, until now, I was never home during most daylight hours so coming home for the day was new to me. I was not alone as my aging and ailing mother now lived with us, but even she was different now that dementia was slowly reframing her mind. Every now and then we had some lucid conversations, but they were, for the most part, overcome by many more conversations of her questioning me about odd things and random thoughts. She would ask constantly about where her purse was and why we hid the phone from her. Also, with me now spending more time in the house, there seemed to be no lack of home projects to do. Frankly though, most times I did not feel like cleaning out the closets, cabinets or the garage. Heck, I didn't feel like washing the dishes and some days, I didn't feel like washing myself. It was just a continuous blur of thinking about what I used to do.

This seemingly powerless period of time reminded me of the way I felt the year before when I thought I would lose my mother after she had suffered her third heart attack. God had taken her through so much with the first two, so much so that I almost felt greedy asking Him to save her one more time. But when the doctors connected her to the automated external defibrillator (AED) to revive her as I stood outside the hospital room door, the only prayer I could lift up to God was, "Please Lord, not now, I am not ready to lose her." Since I had witnessed her health declining in recent years, I probably should have been more sensitive to this being her "time," but my heart was heavy with the thought of losing her. Selfish, I know, but God knows me and I was not ready to feel the ache of not having my mother in my life however limited her quality of life would be.

Now here I am feeling this same distraught feeling, except it is not a potential loss, it is a real loss. What am I going to do now Lord? How are we going to pay the mortgage? Our bills? Who am I now? I loved the people I had worked with. After 11 years of leading my team, they were like family. I probably spent as much time with them as I did with my own family. It was hard to reframe those relationships into a past tense. As I looked ahead, I wondered how I could make the best of this new time on my hands.

I have never *not* had a job since I was 15 years old. My first job was at a shoe store and it taught me humility. This was back in the day when the salesperson physically measured your foot for fit and kneeled down in front of you and put the potential new shoe on your foot as you tried it on. Can you imagine trying to squeeze a size 9 shoe on a size 10 foot because the customer insisted their foot could not possibly be a size 10? It makes me think of the time Jesus washed the disciple's feet (John 13:4-5). I have thought of this job many times over my life because it was a humbling experience to serve others in such a tangible way. Admittedly, I can't really say I appreciated the long term aspect of this experience as a teenage shoe salesperson.

Then there was the record store which taught me about business operations and customer service and then ultimately my employment with the federal government. I have always worked somewhere, to my mother's regret. She always felt I could have finished college sooner if I had not started working a "real" job while in school. I didn't feel then like I had an option because I purchased a car to get around and needed to pay the monthly car note. It was during my employment with the government that the seeds were sown that began my career in information technology at 21 years old. Over the many years since my first job, I had never been in a place where I did not have a means to take care of myself, but here I was. My own work history was part of the reason it was so hard to wrap my head around my new status. I felt like I have been cast off onto the island of misfit lives.

What was I feeling?

As is the case whenever you face a new, unknown season, you begin to worry about what comes next. Because of my faith, I have always faced challenges with a hopeful anticipation, almost with a "bring it on" attitude, but this was different. I was older and now had a family that depended on my income to support our obligations and lifestyle. I have never been a huge risk-taker (I like to know what I know) so as my life settled into the predictable path I had been on, I realized I am even more risk averse. I was not old enough for retirement, but it was a bit more competitive out there for seasoned applicants in the job market. Additionally, the skill palette in my industry had changed and I would need some advanced training and certifications to ensure my ability to compete. Though I was open to these things, I would need the benefit of time to complete everything.

My 10-year-old daughter was in a private Christian school she loved. She was thriving, but in the midst of all these changes, I wonder if we would need to move her. We have been pretty good at managing our money, but the unknown is nerve-wracking. It either woke me up in the middle of the night or it kept me from going to sleep altogether. It distracted me in conversations with people. I should have been coasting towards that rocking chair on the beach of retirement, but instead, a giant wave had come and taken everything out into the ocean. These were the thoughts that were going through my head at the time. I gave no consideration to the fact my husband was working and we had savings to subsist on for a while.

More importantly, though I trusted God for our provision and direction, the role He played in these events and the future were not at the forefront of any of 'my' plans.

I would pray to Him for direction and comfort but never thought this could be a stepping stone on His path for my life. One key dilemma for me during this post *Event* season was I would say I trusted God, but now that my back was against the (now crumbling) wall I found myself worrying quite a bit. I started asking myself, "Do I really trust Him?" and was concerned that my answer was not a confident one. When you are dealing with a familiar recipe, it is easy to have trust. It takes a different kind of trust when you are working with partial ingredients. When the formula you have always known is compromised, how can you be sure of the outcome? When the store has run out of milk and eggs and you need to make the cake right now - can you really even call the final product a cake? How can I support my family with no income? Though I never thought this season would last very long, I was in an unfamiliar place. Remember, I have had a paycheck since I was 15 years old. Being unemployed was disorienting after working for so many years.

We had just started attending a new church where my husband and I intentionally chose to take a lower profile role from the visible, front row positions we had in our previous church. I am an ordained minister and welcomed the opportunity to worship anonymously during this time without having to encourage others while feeling defeated at the same time. I have learned though, you are never really anonymous in the Christian faith – God will always require you to share your testimony with others, even when you don't feel like it. This was no exception for me during this time as it seemed everyone I ran into or met wanted to know about my life, job, health (because I had lost weight from not eating), my plan for world peace (said sarcastically), my plans for tomorrow...whatever. It seemed I was put in a position where I had to share. I guess that is what true faith is all about. Always being prepared to talk about how God is going to get you through even though I had no idea how He was going to do it.

Even though I sought God for wisdom and direction, it seemed all of my prayers always ended with me whining about my finances and future. At the time of my departure, my previous employer was stretched financially. As a result, I was not given a severance. I left with only my faith and memories in tow. I have this visual from the movie "The Ten Commandments" in my mind when the Israelites were complaining to Charlton Heston (I mean Moses) about how they were going to make bricks for Pharaoh with no straw (Exodus 5). Every prayer always led to me bemoaning the fact that my mortgage had far more lifespan than my available 'straw' supply (savings) and possibly touching the unavailable straw (my retirement savings and investments).

Whine, whine, whine....I didn't take into account that it was God who had provided the means to both streams of income in the first place.

Interestingly, in this same passage of Scripture even Moses questioned God on His motives about his own God-given mission to get Pharaoh to free the Israelites from the bondage of slavery in Egypt. The Israelites only bore wrath from Pharaoh since Moses had arrived and began imploring Pharaoh to release them. Moses began asking God "Why have you sent me to do this thankless job?" (Exodus 5:22) And now here I am, like Moses, playing the blame game because these resulting events from my termination are causing discomfort for me. I began second-guessing every decision I made at my previous company and wondering whether they may have led to my current situation - even though they were made for the right reasons. I was not remembering that I also sought God's direction before making many of the decisions that I was now questioning - for example, taking on new office space as the company grew and going after strategic work that took more upfront investment before seeing greater profit returns in the longer term.

It is sometimes hard to accept and keep moving through when you don't have all of the understanding of your future and what to do next. Living in the "valley" can sometimes feel just like the Israelites making those bricks without all of the required ingredients. It is hard and seems impossible if we use our own reasoning. We don't understand how any of this is going to change in the short and possibly longer term. Guess what? You don't have to understand it all. God does.

What does God say?

In looking at those early days of the detour in my life, I was oblivious to the promises of God's provision and presence all around me. I imagine Joseph may have felt the same way. I never stopped praying and probably sought God more than ever before. I found myself literally begging God to change things – right now! Take this hurt away, God. God, can you show me the plan (or winning lottery numbers) in my dreams? I will be obedient and do wherever I need to for my instant blessing. I looked to God as my unicorn, my Santa Clause, my provider, but in all the wrong ways.

What do you think Joseph felt as he sat in prison? He was there so long he was given work to do by the prison warden. (Genesis 39:20-21) There is not a lot of information in Genesis 39 about Joseph's early time in prison or details about what he was feeling emotionally or spiritually. What is clear are the words listed at the end of verse 20 and the beginning of verse 21 – be careful as you read these verses because you may miss it:

"But while Joseph was there in the prison, the LORD was with him"

Read that beginning part of verse 21 slowly to yourself, *"the Lord was with him."* Joseph was still in prison but God reminds us, as we read about his life, that He was with Joseph in the pit of that prison. It even goes on to say that God's favor was with Joseph. I'm sure if Joseph was asked about this he might have preferred God's favor be *outside* the prison walls. I know I would. But when I read this, it reminds me that no matter where we are in life – the top or the bottom – God is there. God is there! He is not bound by our circumstances or physical boundaries because He is everywhere. You are not alone. I was not alone. Even as I sat in my involuntary, self-imposed prison of disorienttation, God was with me. He knew what I was going through and what I was feeling. He heard my spoken and unspoken prayers. More than anything, He knew the heartache I was feeling. Psalm 56:8 says God keeps track of all of our sorrows and "[God] has collected all of my tears in [his] bottle." When I read this, I see the actions of a loving Father tending to His hurting child. How comforting this thought is. Though I can't necessarily say I felt God's presence in such a visibly peaceful way during this time - because the unknown was making my worry louder than my peace - it is a promise that lets us in on His character and care for His children. We are His flock. Little did I know how much I would need this comfort, but I have come to realize now how God was right there with me all the time.

Guess what: He is with you, too! Sometimes we can get so caught up in what we are feeling that we don't acknowledge (or care) that God already knows what we are going through. Do you think Joseph cared that God was with him? We can't really tell from Scripture, but one thing we do know, Joseph remained in prison. He had favor but his outward circumstances did not change.

Why do you think the Bible would mention he had favor when he was still in an undesirable situation? Stay tuned as we forge on in this story because I think God wants us to remember that He is with us, just like He was with Joseph. We are not left forsaken or abandoned. God meets us where we are.

Redeemed Reflections

Don't Worry, Be Happy?

The more I worried about what might happen (or not happen) tomorrow, the more depressed I got. I was reminded of the time I was a Deacon in my previous church and we had to memorize Scriptures to encourage others when they were going through tough times. Since money and health were consistent topics when I ministered, I memorized the Scriptures on worry in Matthew 6. Now here I was, worrying, and these Scriptures never crossed my mind. I should add this caveat; they never crossed my mind *until* I was in random places like Starbucks or picking my daughter up from school. I'd be going about my business and a sparrow would just fly out of nowhere and land in front of me. This made me think of my mother's favorite song *His*

Eye is On the Sparrow and the verse, "and I know He watches over me." I'd be sitting in my car, daydreaming (worrying) and staring out of the window, tears welling up in my eyes and boom! Another sparrow would just land on the roof of my car. And, when I looked closer, it would have food in its mouth! This happened more times than I could count. Maybe it wasn't happenstance, maybe God just gave me a greater sensitivity to what was already a normal part of life (which it is) but who knew these little sparrows were all over the place like they were. So now I started listening –

Matthew 6:25-27 says:

"Therefore I tell you, do not worry about your life, what you will eat or drink; or about your body, what you will wear. Is not life more than food, and the body more than clothes? Look at the birds of the air; they do not sow or reap or store away in barns, and yet your heavenly Father feeds them. Are you not much more valuable than they? Can any one of you by worrying add a single hour to your life?"

Huh? God, I am not sure I know how to live free like a sparrow and to not worry. It sure is easier when there is a paycheck coming into the bank account. Our culture teaches us to worry – to focus on the problem at hand. Many drugs in the pharmaceutical industry are founded in helping us through our worry. The devil would prefer we worry than rely on God. I don't know how *not* to worry. Then God says in verse 34:

Therefore do not worry about tomorrow, for tomorrow will worry about itself. Each day has enough trouble of its own."

I found myself negotiating with God saying, "Okay, God – I'm going to try this your way. I am going to try to focus on today only, seeking You first but I am really going to need You to help me keep my mind off tomorrow because believe me – it is not natural for me. Help me please!"

God's Timing and Actions Will Make No Sense to Us

As I am writing this book, I am approaching my 22nd wedding anniversary. The first 10 years of my marriage, my husband and I were considered "DINKS" – Dual Income, No Kids. It was not for lack of wanting a child, we *really* wanted many children, but as the years went on we started to think it was not our lot in life to be parents. We looked at adoption, but as we settled on a sibling pair to adopt, the grandmother of the children decided she wanted to raise them so that option faded quickly. One day, unexpectedly, the Holy Spirit urged me to go through one more In Vitro Fertilization (IVF) cycle. I was hesitant as it would be my third attempt and I just could not handle another disappointment. So I tested God to make sure everything lined up according to my plan before I would try. Amazingly, it did – the timing of the initial consultation and appointments, the financial commitment needed, my husband was not traveling as much and I, for the first time in my career, had some flexibility in my schedule to deal with the untimely administration of the medication and potential side effects. God surely was letting me know this was it! He was setting the stage for a miracle, right?

Once the process was complete, I took a pregnancy test at the appropriate time. As I stood in the bathroom looking at that test, there was no plus sign, no minus sign – nothing. I interpreted this as a negative response and I was so angry I threw it into the trash can and cursed God for making me feel this heartache again. I could actually feel a swelling pain in my chest as I pleaded to God to stop leading me on if He was not going to bless us. I'll admit, I sounded a little like Moses in my despair as I questioned God's intentions. It was too painful to hope for something like parenthood only to have God not deliver on this request. Have you ever felt that kind of grief when expecting something from God? He must not love me if He continues to allow me to experience this discomfort, right? As I sat down on the floor and cried my eyes out I suddenly heard a voice say, "You did not wait long enough!" It was so startling that I turned around to see if my husband had come into the room. Interestingly, it was not my high pitched voice I heard, but a deep booming voice. We always wonder what a 'God-Encounter' would be like and I think this was mine. After I calmed down a bit, I reached into the trash can and pulled the pregnancy test out and there right before my eyes was the most beautiful sign ever… a pink sign. I was finally pregnant!

God's timing will never make sense to us, but it is perfect. My husband and I went through 10 years of longing to be parents before God granted our wish and it was not the regular path many take to become parents. If I was not obedient when the idea popped into my mind about the third IVF cycle, we may not be parents now.

Isaiah 55:8-9 says:

> "For my thoughts are not your thoughts, neither are your ways my ways, saith the LORD. For as the heavens are higher than the earth, so are my ways higher than your ways, and my thoughts than your thoughts."

So here I sit these many years later, going through another season where I am looking to God for my deliverance and I am once again needing to rely on my faith. I have a living, breathing example of what He can do in front of me every day in my daughter Madison, yet I am still anxious. I ask God to give me the strength to keep looking up to Him, even if I don't quite understand what He is trying to do in my life.

Find Your Place

To clear my mind, I walked a lot during the initial days and weeks following *The Event*. Not very far distances and with no particular goal in mind. Actually, I'm just trying not to lose my mind. I walked and prayed. I prayed and walked. In the warmth of late summer, in the coolness of fall, in the cold of winter, I walked. I walked around the same exact block in my neighborhood one time, two times, three times. Each turn around the block was exactly one mile. I went around again and again and again. And God spoke to me. Much of what you will read in this book came from Him during my walks. The most important message I received was a dictate to remind people (including me) that He is always with us and knows what we go through. This is where I heard the subtle suggestion to write this book. It was not until a year later that I learned to appreciate my place in relationship to God, His timing, and His purpose. One day, God opened my eyes after a particularly whiny walk around the block. It was as if He said, "Look at what I have done for you every time you walked this block and talked to Me."

I instantly understood my arrogance. So many blessings had come into my life and I was still questioning His involvement in my current situation. The following is a small sampling of the things I have prayed about over the two decades we have lived in this particular neighborhood – the things I worried about or celebrated while walking this very same block:

- Should I take this CEO job?
- Direction for my job/Protection from my job

- The journey of infertility (every Mother's Day, I walked)
- The joy of being pregnant
- Gotta get this pregnancy weight off
- Dad is sick
- Mom is sick
- Grieving
- Mad with my husband
- Happy with my husband
- Cover my daughter
- Cover my marriage
- Yay – Madison accepted you as Savior
- Oops– bank account is low
- We need a new refrigerator
- Prayers for others/Thanksgiving for answered prayers
- And now – next steps after losing my job

The list goes on....

Find your place. It may be your bedroom, the park, a chapel or the neighboring coffee shop. This block holds my tears, fears, dreams, curses – everything. It reminds me that I still stand. You need a place that is your sacred quiet place to spend time with God. Sometimes, we are told that our "place" should be a quiet spot somewhere inside. But this block I walk, outside in the Glory of God's creation, it holds my deepest feelings and secrets – and my most sacred conversations with a loving, listening God.

Find your safe place and take everything to the Savior – He is waiting.

Really God? Digging Ditches in the Valley

Chapter 3

Dear God –

I am wondering if you are hearing me. I guess if I have to be imprisoned, I should not complain because it seems the warden trusts me and is treating me pretty well. That being said, I am still in prison. Now he is making me the caretaker of these two new characters that just showed up – the Pharaoh's Cupbearer and his Baker. How in the world did they end up here? They have the easiest jobs in the world – who messes up that type of job?! What could they have done to end up in prison with me? Maybe Potiphar's wife was on the prowl again. I don't know, but I will do my best as always. It would be great if you could you send me a little sign that the end is near? I am starting to forget about who I was and what I used to do. Maybe I really do deserve this punishment.

Oh well God, good talking to you.

Love, Joseph

Warning: This chapter is an emotionally tough one. It is one that captures a myriad of feelings that go beyond *The Event*. This chapter rounds out the true passion that forms the foundation of this book.

This chapter is about my mother.

But first, let me give you some perspective of the timeframe of events since Chapter 1. *The Event* happened in the heat of the summer in the latter part of July and I am now almost 2 weeks into my new season. I am still feeling a little lost but am trying to accommodate the change by filling the day with busyness. Today, in addition to accessing the job market, I was busy cleaning out old mail and papers that needed to be shredded. I was busy going through my daughter's clothes to find out what she has outgrown so we can donate it. I was busy sorting my massive piles of books so I can take a trip to the library to get rid of them. The one problem with these tasks was I was filtering and sorting and cleaning, but the resulting piles all seemed to end up in the garage. All work, but no definitive action. I was not ready to go out and face a world that was available at 11:00 a.m. in the morning. Before losing my job, I was never available at 11:00 a.m. in the morning. I usually did this stuff on the weekends. I was now coming to the realization that busyness does not fix any problems – it just delays the inevitable confrontation with them.

Even though I wasn't working, I would get up because staying in bed seemed to make me feel worse. I avoided what I was feeling inside emotionally as much as I could. I think my family was relieved I was avoiding any topics surrounding *The Event* because they would not have to deal with my emotional state of mind. As my daughter would say later, "we all were walking around softly to keep Mommy from blowing up." For the record, holding your emotions inside and not addressing them is NOT a good way to handle your feelings. They will come out one way or another. But I digress...

I mentioned earlier that my aging mother was now living with me. She is not independent in her living but thankfully she is able to do the more personal things for herself like going to the bathroom, and dressing and feeding herself. She really cannot be left alone because she is considered legally blind. I have been amazed at what she can do with her self-described, "blind in one eye and can't see in the other" status. Somehow, she still reads the newspaper every morning and looks at the news and her favorite show, *The Price is Right.* She uses a cane to get around but I am convinced she uses it more for sight than stability. Whatever works, I guess.

The reason I ultimately had to move Mom in with me was because her many heart ailments finally caught up with her. After her aortic aneurysm surgery was done three years ago, I picked her up from the hospital and brought her to my home to recover. After that, she never went back to her own home. My father was still living at the time and was none too happy his wife was now living with me. God, in His wisdom, knew what was coming as my father had a stroke some months later and ended up living with my brother. When I think about that time, I thank God for family and the ability to be there for our parents.

When I was working, I had an elder care nurse come in and take care of Mom during the day. She was an awesome soul who cared for Mom with the same loving touch I would give her. I never had a care in the world when I was away – I could travel to my company's other office locations or go out with the family for the night without any concerns. My mother's nurse, Caroline, was readily there.

Until she was not…

Earlier in the summer, Caroline had mentioned she needed to take a sabbatical to visit her family in another country for a month. At the time, I could only run through my mind how long a month was and what would I do for Mom's care during that time. I know, this was selfish as she needed to see her family too, but it made me anxious because I really did not have a backup plan. The fact was, I had never allowed a replacement nurse to come in when Caroline was absent because it seemed to cause some confusion for Mom as her aging mind made her wary of strangers and change. Thinking about a month's absence at that time was causing me some stress. When would she be leaving? The first week of August. What time is it now? The first week of August.

In light of my new availability, I now became my mother's full-time caregiver.

What was I feeling?

Ahh....the dynamics of a mother/daughter relationship. They can be loving but complex at the same time - so I will leave that to another book. The interactions and demands between mother and daughter can be simultaneously enriching and draining. The interactions when the daughter is the caregiver? Complicated is the only word that comes to mind. I had a wonderful relationship with my mother, especially after I got older. She became my confidante, my advisor, my friend and ultimately my 'to do' buddy. We would go to the store together or just hang out doing nothing at all. I learned the most about my family's history when we were just riding around town. Before she became ill, she and my father would catch a bus to the neighboring casino with all of the other seniors in the community. Though not my preference for her spare time, I realized it kept her busy and engaged with others. She was very active in her church and her faith gave her a keen sense of responsibility so she didn't spend her entire retirement on the penny slot machines. I think her fervor for going to the casino was bested only by one other thing – going to Walmart. We used to call her 'Wal-Mary' (because her name was Mary). She loved to go there and walk the aisles. We would debate constantly whether she really needed another pair of socks or a giant bottle of lotion. She believed you couldn't pass these things up because the price was so reasonable. She loved that place!

As her sight faded, I decided it may be a bit unsafe for her and Dad to go to the casino on a bus with strangers so I offered to drive them there. In my mind, it offered a way to keep an eye on them. Because Dad's knees were causing him some problems in walking, he eventually stopped going so it just became Mom and me. Though she did not mind, her only requirement of me was that I don't tell her what to do with her money. Okay. Hard to do, but I complied.

I can never place a value on the blessing of those times in the car with Mom. We became two peas in a loving pod. And now here I am taking care of my pod-mate who, by the way, has now also become increasingly cranky in her older years. Was Mom always this stubborn when it came to her selection of food? Why is it a negotiation every time she needs take her medicine? This sweet little lady just told me to get the heck out of her room – she can pick her own clothes out. Who is she?

That August month of caring for Mom was fraught with feelings of being thankful, that I could be here for her during the winter season of her life, amid feelings of anxiety on what's next for me. How perfect of God to free up my schedule just in time for Caroline's sabbatical. This period of my life was also filled with ponderings of when God was going to release me so I can get back to my true calling in business and let Caroline get back to hers on her return from visiting family. In my mind, I was only going to be around for a short period of time so I did not want to get too used to this daytime caregiving role. God surely had a new job waiting for me. I think the daily visual of seeing my once strong and courageous mother turning into a person who was increasingly dependent on others for her care was pulling on every emotion within me. Caregiving was draining my spirit.

    I love my mother dearly but on the coattails of losing my job, this new responsibility was bittersweet. In hindsight, I would not have had it any other way – my mother was my most precious responsibility in addition to my daughter and husband. But to be honest, taking care of another individual when you are yearning for care yourself is very challenging. I began to question God's timing. I could handle any one of these things individually, but not both at the same time. There is no word to describe the heaviness I felt inside.

What does God say?

When looking at the experience of Joseph in our Scripture, nothing had really changed for him – he was still in prison and now he had the responsibility of caring for other prisoners. When you read this in Scripture, it almost seems like Joseph should have been grateful. After all, he had authority (however limited) over his new cellmates and he had favor from the warden who pretty much left him alone. We should keep in mind, Joseph did not have the benefit of seeing how this story was going to end like we do. He was living it in real time. His faith was being tested. The life that Joseph knew had changed and he did not really know what was coming next.

What do you think Joseph was feeling? I would imagine that he saw other prisoners come and go and he was still left there. Remember, he was falsely accused of his crime so I would imagine, in his humanity, he felt everything he was going through was pretty unfair. Do you think he felt isolated? How about discouraged and maybe even confused? Now he was expected to care for others while figuring out how to care for himself. These are feelings we all can probably relate to.

What about Joseph's prison mates? Do you think they looked at him like he should not complain? He *was* the wardens chosen pet at the time. I'm sure it seemed like a pretty good position to be in compared to the other prisoners. I think Joseph kept a lot bottled up inside of himself because he felt he had no right to grumble compared to others.

In Scripture, there are many stories of God using mere mortals like ourselves when they were in the wilderness (or imprisoned) times of life. He used Joseph to minister to others amid his own trial. We never see him question or complain to God, he just served where he was. I must admit, this approach was a little harder for me, initially. But as I delved more into Scripture during this season, I realized that complaining and questioning were getting me absolutely nowhere. It didn't even make me feel better. I could hear Dr. Phil's signature phrase in my ear every time I complained saying, "How is that working out for you?" It was, quite frankly, not working out for me at all. I realized I had to step back and look at the bigger picture.

God had Joseph (and me and you) in this place for a reason.

God does His best teaching in the wilderness.

Rather than be frustrated with the *why* maybe we should ask *what* He needs for us to do while here. For me, I knew I had to give my mother the best care I could even though, at first, I really wasn't up to the task. I can't tell you how many times I asked God *why* He was making me do this. Like Joseph, I did not have the benefit of the whole story. But I have come to realize – God does.

Redeemed Reflections

The Elephant in the Room

When people of faith go through tough seasons I think it is easy to wonder *where is God* during the hard times? I know I called out to God so many times to take away my discomfort that I would playfully think that He might have my prayers blocked so He could deal with other people's requests. For me, the elephant in the room was God's grace. It was right there. It *is* right there for all of us - available to us every moment but so very hard to feel when hurt and tears speak louder than our faith. I would cry out, *Take it God – you own the cattle on a thousand hills remember?* I cried out so much that I sometimes had to laugh at myself on how pitiful it probably sounded. Then God reminded me, my crying out was nothing new. In the New Testament, the Apostle Paul asked God to remove a condition from him which God allowed to remain (2 Corinthians 12:8-9). The condition is never revealed, so I substituted my own state every time I read this passage. When I did this, it gave me the same perspective I believe Paul received.

Paul understood that God's grace is truly sufficient. One of the hardest lessons to learn in life is contentment with where we are. Grace in contentment teaches us about peace and joy in spite of our circumstances. We learn to be sensitive to all areas where God is working in our lives. It allows us to go through our "prison times" with strength. We also learn about our strength compared to God's power. During these periods, God does not take time off in leading our lives - He is still writing your story. Joseph was learning, though he probably could not see it, that this season was all a part of the purpose God had in mind for him. It was a chapter in the book of his life. 2 Corinthians 12:8-9 says (with my comment):

Concerning (Insert Your Situation Here), I pleaded with the Lord three times that it might depart from me. And He said to me, "My grace is sufficient for you, for My strength is made perfect in weakness." Therefore most gladly I will rather boast in my infirmities, that the power of Christ may rest upon me.

As you journey through life, you need a game plan to deal with the unexpected events that come along the way, especially those things that endure for a season longer than you anticipated. Though the entire Bible provides an abundance of guidance on this topic, the following are some steps to encourage you to keep going - to fully understand that "God's grace (truly) is sufficient" for whatever it is we will face as we journey along life's pathways.

Steps to Keep Going

- Remember – life is a puzzle. Like a puzzle, every piece contributes to the final creation.

- To God, no part of life is meant to be a destination - Keep running the race of life.

- Avoid having a pity party at all costs. Feel your feelings but keep moving. When you stop at the weigh station of guilt, loneliness or bitterness it will only open a door for separation and disobedience from God. Keep moving – your life depends on it.

- God is the author and finisher of our faith (Hebrews 12:2). He is also the author and finisher of our story – give the pen to Him and let Him keep writing.

- Like Joseph, we still have favor even in our "prisons."

- God's grace is sufficient and there is nothing new to Him. He knows what you are going through.

Postscript on Being Content:

It took me some time to realize I was grieving a job that for the most part was stressing me out greatly. In the years leading up to *The Event* my quality of life had suffered due to my absence in my family's life. We rarely had family dinners together except on special occasions and I could not get past this continual pain in my stomach which was later determined to be a small ulcer. As you just read, I was crying over a job that probably was impacting my personal relationships and health more than I was willing to admit. Though I thrived off the challenges it would bring, what I did not realize was one of the main relationships it had impacted was my relationship with God. Other than Sunday, I had stopped doing weekly Bible study and outreach ministry because my work hours had gotten longer and longer. Other than a few drive-by prayers with my family, my prayer life was devoted to the time it took to commute to and from work in my car. The quality of life of the individuals connected to me was not quality at all. My daughter was always the last one to be picked up from school aftercare and why was I always rushing to get there?

As you continue to read my story, think about your own journey. Think about *The Events* of your life. Outside of the ones you can't control totally like a health diagnosis or other people's actions - Do you ever find yourself holding onto things that may meet some needs but don't give you peace? Do they impact your ability to experience the abundance that comes from living in the content spirit of God's provision? If so, ask the Lord for direction on what to do about them. He already knows what you are going through and He is a "yoke-bearing" God. He asks you to let Him help you carry some of these things – this way He can guide you to that peaceful place. The place He says is beyond our understanding.

"And the peace of God, which transcends all understanding, will guard your hearts and your minds in Christ Jesus"

Philippians 4:7

Empty

Chapter 4

Dear God –

First, I want to say hello and I am grateful for the ability to talk to you. If it was not for your presence, I think I would lose my mind in this place. Something kind of weird just happened. I don't know if it is the prison food or something else, but the King's Cupbearer and the Baker both had some really, interesting dreams last night. It bothered them so much they could only sit around sadly trying to figure out what the dreams meant. Since you gave me this gift of also dreaming some pretty elaborate dreams, I am coming to you to see what it all means. I have to admit though, I am a bit wary – it was, after all, me telling my brothers about my dreams that landed me in that pit and ultimately being sold into slavery to Potiphar. I guess since I didn't die in the pit I should be thankful though my life is not looking that great right now. Anyway, if you can tell me what their dreams mean maybe I can provide some relief to their souls.

I have not told you lately God, but thanks for always being there.

Love, Joseph

It is November 21st and we are running around getting the house ready for the upcoming Thanksgiving holiday. What a blessing it is to be distracted for a moment thinking about this holiday. Because of my mother's health, I have slowed down the process of looking for full time employment so I could focus on her care. Mom's hospitalization a couple of weeks ago was scary but I am glad I made the decision for her not to have surgery to correct the potential swelling of her aortic aneurysm. From previous experience with her, I really did not want her to go through this surgery again. At her age, I was not sure she could handle the surgery (or recovery) and I am coming to the regretful place of accepting whatever is God's will as it relates to her health.

As I am cleaning the kitchen, my husband Garry suddenly comes running into the kitchen to tell me Mom is upstairs complaining about being in pain and not feeling well. I rush upstairs only to find her sitting on the edge of her bed moaning that she is uncomfortable and needs to go to the hospital – now!

My mother is pretty resilient so her asking me to take her to the hospital meant she was not only feeling bad, she felt like (excuse the adjective) crap. She hated going to the doctor so asking me to take her there meant whatever she was feeling she wanted it to stop immediately. I decide to drive her to the hospital myself since it is not that far and within minutes we are in the car and off we go. She was just at this particular hospital recently, so it did not take long for them to find her records and review test results. The doctors on duty take note of the aneurysm diagnosis but ask if they can do another x-ray to see if it had burst. I replied, meekly, "I guess, okay," while wondering if I made the wrong decision last time. Maybe we should have gotten that surgery? Now I am the total opposite of the last visit and find myself begging them to do whatever they needed to do. Get Mom better – please!

As I sit in the emergency room once again, I can't think straight. Now I was questioning God – Why? What did I do to get here? I can handle my issues, but I don't think I can handle the crisis of my mother's failing health at the same time. I glance over to her as she lay so helplessly in bed. She was in pain and was literally begging me to get the doctors to do something to stop the discomfort in her stomach. They wanted to wait until the x-ray results came back before administering any medicine so I was left to hold her hand, catch her vomit, clean her up and see that discouraging look in her eyes questioning why I was letting this happen to her. Why was I letting the doctors ignore her request for pain medicine? We waited and waited and waited.

Finally, the attending doctor comes back in with some surprising news. In looking at her current x-rays there didn't appear to be a problem with her aorta. No aneurysm at all - it looked fine. It also looked fine in her previous x-rays from what they could tell. As a matter of fact, it was not clear what was causing her pain. Her feeble heart was as strong as it could be considering her age and medical history and all of her vital signs were not a cause for concern. As with all senior patients, she was slightly dehydrated so they were going to put her on an IV and...(this is how it all sounded to me)...blah...blah...blah – I was still stuck on the *we don't see a problem with the aorta* part. I began to think about all of the what ifs? What if I consented to the surgery before? Especially since it *now* appears she didn't need the surgery. What if she had died? I am confused with this news. What is going on? God – What is happening?

At that moment, I realized how grateful I was that I could be there for Mom.

How glad I was to be there to make decisions for her and to pray for and with her. I know she would have consented to the surgery previously if I had not been there.

It was God's wisdom while praying the last time she was hospitalized that told me not to agree to the recommended surgery. She is still very uncomfortable but I have decided to hold true to my decision of doing nothing extraordinary that would make her more uncomfortable unless there is a real reason to do so. I tell them to please help her with her pain and then we can discuss next steps.

Mom was moved to a critical care room from the emergency room to determine what was causing her so much discomfort. Once she arrived in the room she had calmed down somewhat and the medicine she was given for her pain and nausea helped tremendously.

Two days and many tests later, two of her doctors requested a meeting with me to discuss her care plan. Because I had decided against any surgery, it appeared they were at a loss on what to do with her though they were in agreement that she was very weak and something was going on that needed attention.

When we met, Doctor #1 (who was one of her cardiologists) told me that her heart was very weak and she was only using 20 percent of her heart capacity. After the damage of three heart attacks, she was considered a congestive heart patient for much of the last decade so this was not surprising news. My nickname for her was Lazarette (like Lazarus in the Bible) because it seemed she kept getting up after each heart ailment. I have always been amazed at what she could do with that little piece of heart she was working with. Only God knows how she has been able to last this long.

Doctor #2, of the unpleasant news tag team, looked at me and said they really are not sure why my mother is so uncomfortable. The thought is she is getting older and her body just may be slowing down.

I sat and listened.

Doctor #1 said, "There is not much more we can do and in looking at her health, she may not have much more time left."

I asked, "When you say time are you referencing....life?"

Doctor #1 said, "Yes."

I asked, "How much time are we talking?"

"We don't know. It could be 3 months, it could be 6 months or even longer. We just don't know."

I started tearing up. Even though I had anticipated this season of her life coming, I had never had it verbalized as an inevitable event before now. I knew it would happen, but....

I asked, "What should I do until then? What happens next?"

Doctor #2 jumped in, as if on cue, and pulled a folder out to go over the requirements of hospice care with me.

As she went on and on I cannot really say I was listening. There was that word hospice; it made me squirm in my seat.

And just like that, five minutes later my mother was categorized as a hospice patient and we started planning her discharge and further care plans once she returned home.

The doctors left me alone for a minute to think about things. I cried and prayed for strength and understanding. All I could muster up when they came back in to see if I had any questions, was to request they disconnect her pacemaker before she was discharged. Since she was so weak, the thought of it kicking in for its intended purpose, to jumpstart her heart with a shock if it ever stopped, only made me feel more discouraged.

What was I feeling?

Helpless is the only descriptor I can come up with when thinking about this time. I know I am not the first child to go through this with their parent and won't be the last. A dire prognosis presents a helpless state for anyone providing care to someone they love. Why? Because there is nothing we can do but love and support them. I was proud of being able to care for my mother as it showed her that she had done well in raising me. But I had to admit to myself, I really did not want to walk this long road to her impending transition. Emotionally, I was beaten down and spiritually, I began to hear silence. Silence. The God who had spoken to me so boldly when I was trying to have my daughter was not saying anything. No hallowed voice. Nothing. Why would God be silent during a time like this? I began to refer to this time period as the "empty season" because as much as I called on God, nothing could take away the void inside of me. I was exhausted mentally, emotionally and physically.

Somehow, The Event continued to seem smaller and smaller.

When I was in that hospital, I realized my real mission in life was to be there for my mother and to be her advocate. It also became clear the path I was on was illuminated by God. Sure, with the added stress of losing an income and all that comes with it, this would not have been the script I would have written for my life but I now know - God knows better.

I think God went silent during this time (and many times since) because He knew there was nothing He could have said that would have made me feel any better. If an angel came into my room shouting, *I am here child – Trust Me!* it would not have taken away the fear and grief I was beginning to feel about losing my mother. Knowing she was going to die, what could He have said? *We've got a nice place here in heaven waiting just for her?* Nope, that would not have worked. So blindly I went through the motions, in my empty state, beginning the process of setting up a comfortable place at home for Mom when she is discharged from the hospital.

A couple of days pass and Mom is now coming home, just in time for Thanksgiving. That verse in the Bible that says God won't give you more than you can handle is in my spirit for some reason (1 Corinthians 10:13). I am not really feeling its meaning right now as I don't want to handle another thing and anyway, Paul was talking about being tempted, not suffering. This is something I did not choose.

But - I keep going, amazingly. I guess I am stronger than I think...

What Does God Say?

When issues hit close to home, it is hard to even see God's meaning in them and we may often question if He is even there. The one guarantee we do have when "real" life occurs is that all life will go on. And because this is life - we have no choice but to keep on living.

Keep Living

We can complain and we can whine, but when we stop complaining and whining – our *thing* is still there. For survival, we have to keep moving in the valley because we still have a life to live. We can try to run away from our situations or even try to ignore them, but they are still there. I liken it to having a serious disagreement with your spouse that may leave you both not speaking to each other. If you have kids, you still have to get them ready for bed or school or maybe even help with homework. The conflict is still there awaiting resolution but you still have to face the activities of life. Even in the valley there is still work to do.

Much like Joseph in our Scripture passage, though he was still imprisoned, he is being utilized by the warden of the prison to manage some of the other prisoners and the daily workload. His compassion, in noticing the Cupbearer and the Baker were sad when they had their unusual dreams, probably came from being in such close proximity to them on a day to day basis. I suspect Joseph could empathize with them because the longer he was in prison, he probably wondered if he would ever do the things he did in his previous life again. Now here he was using a gift he probably didn't even think of as a gift; assisting the Cupbearer and Baker with interpreting their dreams. There are times in life when we will go through seasons where we would rather pull the covers over our head in the morning and stay in bed. It is in these moments that we discover what we are made of. That's when we find ourselves working and doing those things necessary for survival *and*, in the process, helping others. God can and will use us for ministry/ fellowship/ service – even if it is at a time we can't even minister to ourselves.

Don't Isolate

I think God makes us look outside ourselves to keep us from looking too hard within. Looking within makes us depressed and frustrated when we think of our challenges (and sometimes failures) in comparison to how He looks at us. After all, our main purpose in this Christian life is to love and lift up others – it is all in the Bible. God knows this is part of the cycle that keeps life in our spirits. Why? Because if we only focus on our failures and struggles, it opens a door for the enemy to get in our heads and start the slow process of separation – separation from family, friends, community and, more specifically, God. Proverbs 18:1 says:

"A man who isolates himself seeks his own desire;

He rages against all wise judgment."

When we are broken, we do broken things. That is why God suggests the community and fellowship of others. If we are the only person we seek for comfort when we feel sad or overwhelmed, it is like rehydrating a sponge with only our tears. There is not enough moisture to bring it back to life. Similarly, looking outside helps us maintain a sense of purpose and accomplishment. Joseph could have chosen not to assist the Cupbearer and the Baker, but I imagine it elevated his psyche a little by helping them to interpret their dreams. Helping and ministering to others really is good for the soul and somehow allows us to take the focus off of our problems, even if it is only for a season. Ministry also broadens our perspective that we are not alone in facing the challenges of life.

Listen and Look out for the Presence of God

There is an aspect of Genesis 40:5-8 that I think we overlook when reading about Joseph – God was silent with him, too. Joseph did not have God-encounters like Moses experienced. No booming voice. No burning bush. We really only see Joseph praying to God. Joseph prayed in faith.

In God's silence, Joseph never lost faith. Joseph had to listen out for God in other ways. God was the first one he turned to when faced with the task of interpreting his prison-mates dreams. We go on to read that God responded to Joseph by giving him the meaning of those dreams, but we don't read that Joseph had a "burning bush" meeting with God in the middle of the night. Joseph just knew God was there. I believe when God seems silent, we need to remember – God is never silent. He is always with us. That is His promise. We just have to look for the other ways He communicates. Guidance only comes when you spend time listening for and to His voice. Joseph did not have a Bible to read like we do now – he had to rely on a place deeper inside his spirit - his faith. Sometimes, those quiet times are the only encouragement we can get when dire events are happening around us.

Take the time to seek God and listen.

Keep looking up!

Redeemed Reflections

Tips for Walking Through the "Empty Season"

- God never gives you more than you can handle – You are stronger than you think (augmented by Jesus' strength) – Philippians 4:13

- "The season you are in today is not your story – it is just a layover" (Steven Furtick, Lead Pastor, Elevation Church, Charlotte, North Carolina)

- Remember - Peace is Possible (Isaiah 26:3). Write this down and put it everywhere!

- Your Faith is your Tool. It is your Power. It is your Comfort. Hold on to it! -2 Thessalonians 1:11

- Though you feel lonely you are not alone. God knows exactly what you are going through. He said he would never leave us or forsake us. He is there.

- Be careful - broken people do broken things. Don't substitute what you feel you are missing with unhealthy replacements. Remember, isolating yourself from others is an unhealthy replacement too. Look out and up!

Postscript:

Like Joseph, God called on me to take care of my mother while still in the grips of my own "prison." He used my love and compassion for her to take my mind off the other troubles in my life. *The Event* was taking on a whole new purpose. I was grateful to be used for her care in such a special way. I would never have been able to take the time off work that was needed to be with her in this final season. Only God could take this empty place I was in and somehow redefine it into ministry. God crafted this season so I could serve my mother during her greatest time of need and transformed my thinking and purpose in the process.

Empty...Continued

Chapter 5

Dear God –

Now I am really confused. What did I do for this to happen? I have not done anything – to my brothers, to Potiphar and *now* the Cupbearer and the Baker have forgotten me! I have only tried to help them - and in prison, I continue to sit. I interpreted their dreams and they *promised* me they would remember me before Pharaoh (the King) when they were released. They were freed in time for Pharaoh's birthday celebration so that should have been a good time to let him know about my dilemma. Though I'm thinking this might not have worked out too well for the Baker (since his dream ended tragically), the Cupbearer surely should have remembered me since I heard he ended up back in the King's good graces. Why am I still here? Why are my deeds returned with such punishment? They were released months ago and nothing has changed.

Why?

I still stand on my faith but people think I'm crazy to trust in *my* God because they are not seeing any results. I'm still holding onto hope but I am weary. Are you listening? Do you care anymore?

Prayerfully, Joseph

It is now the week of Christmas and our family life has changed into something I can only describe as similar to one of those walking zombie movies. We are present but there seems to be no apparent purpose to our movements other than being scared that this might be *the* day. Everything in the house has been modified to account for my mother's care – the furniture, our schedules and even the food we eat. In recent weeks, we also had the untimely experience of my daughter falling in gym class and hitting her head. This accident, unfortunately, resulted in a concussion. Watching two people I love having to struggle with the simple tasks of life drove me tearfully to my knees in prayer. Thankfully, as we enter Christmas week, my daughter is on the mend and in a weird way, her many doctor's appointments provided some needed *outside time* away from the *new normal* in the house. I have not really had time to go shopping for any Christmas gifts (thank you, *Amazon Prime,* for the few gifts I was able to get) and I found myself apologizing to my daughter in advance that this Christmas was going to be different. I am so proud of my little lady (well, maybe not so little as she is ten now) she is really growing into a person that makes me proud especially in her faith walk. She has been the best helper anyone could have and sometimes *she* is the one coming to me to pray for God's help through this new season. I am a big advocate that everyone needs to develop their own personal faith in God, even children, so it pleases me to see hers growing - even under these circumstances. Children growing their own faith and discernment in God is important so they can distinguish the voice of the Holy Spirit from all of the noise of the world. It is so good to see her going to Him boldly as we walk through this desert to a 'known but really unknown' destination.

I have set up camp in the family room which is the room where the family spends most of its time because it has the biggest television. Since I am up and down the steps to my mother's room throughout the day and night, I wanted to be somewhere that would not disturb my family too much, especially at night. My mother's health has taken a sharp decline since she was released from the hospital. Other than juice or water and liquid pain medication, she has had no tangible food since her hospitalization. Initially, I could get her to eat soft foods like yogurt and applesauce but this week she is even turning these offerings down. Her personality is changing as well. All my life I used to call my family a TV sitcom because my mother and father had the best, albeit pretty raw, sense of humor. She could endear you with her quick wit and dry jokes while playing the straight man to my father's jokes. Even with all that she has been through these past months, she never lost her sense of humor – until this week.

This week she has gone radio silent. The only sound in her room is the rhythm of the oxygen machine and the background filler of a television she does not watch anymore.

The hospice nurse came over on the morning of Christmas Eve to check on her status and to let me know they were going to put her on an increased series of the medication she was taking to "keep her comfortable." Based on my observations, that meant "to keep her sleeping" because that is what she did most of the time especially this week. Since being home, a tumor was discovered in her abdomen that we really did not feel until this week. I guess it was visible now because of all of the weight she had lost. In hindsight, that may have been what was causing her the distress she was having during her last hospitalization.

Wearily, I asked, "Why do you need to increase her medication? Does she seem like she is uncomfortable?"

"To keep her comfortable, she does not have much time left," is the response.

I felt like I was in the rerun of a previous viewing of this movie so I asked, "How much time are we talking?"

"She could transition later today or maybe tomorrow."

But, I am thinking, this is Christmas Eve. Not some random day but Christmas Eve?! I think this as if no one ever dies on Christmas Eve....

Now, I cannot take any more. I have reached my limit. My brother is not here yet and now I need to give him a call. I feel bad for my brother because his updates have been relegated to daily text messages, Facetime, and phone calls. Since he lives out of town we agreed that he only needed to come here if Mom's situation became dire. He came home around Thanksgiving, right before she went into hospice, and her current state (with the hospital bed, oxygen tank, and medications) will be a shock for him even though it has been less than a month. I'm sure every time the phone rang he must have panicked wondering if I was calling to tell him something has happened to our mother. Now I have to make the call to tell him this might be that dreaded day we have all been anticipating.

God, how could you take her now? On Christmas Eve? I cannot wrap my head around this possibility even though we have been preparing for it since Thanksgiving. What happened to that three months or more projection?

I just laid my head on the edge of her bed and sobbed without restraint.

What Was I Feeling?

This was such a tough time I had to go back to my journal to see what I wrote during this period in order to write this chapter. I must have been pretty scatterbrained as my daily writings stopped on December 23rd. I guess I did not have it in me. The only thing I found was a post, updating her status, to my family and friends on social media. I must have written it while holding a vigil around my mother's bed on that Christmas Eve.

It said:

As I write this post it is bittersweet. My mom is fading and every moment is truly a gift. When she went into hospice a couple of weeks ago it was hard to accept because she was still her joking and jovial self, albeit very weak. These past couple of days have introduced her to a new and possibly final season. I am realizing that I may not hear her voice again or have an interaction with her, even if it is only her asking for water or to raise the bed. As we are looking to celebrate the birth of Christ, I am reminded that this is what it is all about. When she takes her last breath, Jesus says, "I got this." Though this is not my first encounter with death, there is nothing like a mother's love so it sits really close to my heart. As we enter this Christmas Eve please remember to tell those close to you that you love them because you can never know the timing of their reunion with our Savior. Merry Christmas to you all and I ❤ U.

I sit in wonder as I read this post. Like Joseph, I was still holding onto my God and faith in the middle of this continued state I wished was just a bad dream – like that entire 1985-86 season of the drama *Dallas* where everyone thought the character Bobby was killed in a car accident - only to find out it was all a dream. I want to just wake up and realize this year had just been a bad dream. I love the Lord but have to admit, this was a test I did not want to endure anymore.

What Does God Say?

In Scripture, Joseph, still in prison, appears to have bonded with the Cupbearer and Baker after interpreting their dreams. Though we don't really see it in this passage, I assume it provided them some level of relief to understand what the dreams they had just experienced meant. The exception may have been the Baker, as his dream was somewhat startling and implied he may die after a series of events. This bond seemed enough for Joseph to entrust his fate to them as we read that he asked them to remember to mention his plight to Pharaoh once they were released from prison. There seems to be something sad about this request as it also suggests their imprisonment would only be temporary, while Joseph's seemed indefinite. Sometimes the valley can get so familiar to us we kind of accept our circumstances won't change, especially when there is no clear way out. Scripture does not say specifically how long Joseph was in prison, but we know it was at least two years. Whatever way you look at it, Joseph has been in prison for a long season.

Have any of you felt this way? That no matter how hard you try, you just cannot catch a break? Or maybe, the circumstances you face may be so challenging that you are reaching a point where you just don't want to deal with them anymore.

When you feel this way, my encouragement to you is –

Don't give up.

Don't give in.

Keep the Faith.

Keep Moving.

God is There

There is a little fact in one of the passages we referred to previously that you may miss if you are not paying attention to it. When the Cupbearer and Baker first arrive at the prison, Genesis 40:3-4 says:

[The Cupbearer and Baker were] put in custody in the house of the captain of the guard, in the same prison where Joseph was confined. The captain of the guard assigned them to Joseph, and he attended them.

Who was this 'captain of the guard'? Why it was Potiphar himself. The very same Potiphar that banished Joseph to prison. Why would he give Joseph any responsibility if he did not think positively of his service, work ethic or maybe even his character? He knew Joseph would take care of these highly-esteemed members of the King's court. We don't know why he did not release Joseph if he felt positive thoughts about him but it does not matter because – Joseph had the favor of God.

- Joseph was not your ordinary prisoner, he had supervisory responsibilities. God's Favor.
- Though he could have felt his abilities were fading and useless – the prison warden used him. God's Favor.
- That crazy gift God gave him to interpret dreams, though it did not seem to work out for him with his brothers was now being used in this prison he is in. God's Favor.
- The fact that the Cupbearer and Baker were assigned to Joseph personally by Potiphar. God's Favor.

When you are in the heat of the valley, it makes no sense why things happen the way they do but try to step back and see every event as a piece of a much larger puzzle. Though I did not relish going through the actual task of watching my mother's life fade away, being there for her is something I would not have traded for the world. Though I did not see it while in the middle of the experience, I had God's favor too! Find God's comfort and strength for every step you need to take. God promised us His presence in all that we face or do.

"When thou passest through the waters, I will be with thee; and through the rivers, they shall not overflow thee: when thou walkest through the fire, thou shalt not be burned; neither shall the flame kindle upon thee." Isaiah 43:2

"And let us not grow weary while doing good, for in due season we shall reap if we do not lose heart." Galatians 6:9

Redeemed Reflections

Steps For When the Valley Seems Endless

- Though you may not see it, God is still moving and directing your life.
- Don't lose heart – better yet, give Him your heart! God will take care of you in the middle of the valley.
- Be Obedient – no matter how hard it seems to do so.
- Do good and serve others, no matter how you feel. It is easy to be angry or frustrated but this does more damage to the 'vessel it is stored on than the vessel it is poured on'.
- God is your strength even when you have no strength.
- Don't give up. God still has a plan for you.
- God perfects and strengthens you in your struggles (1 Peter 5:10).

Just God and Me

(Heaven is Looking Pretty Good Right Now)

Chapter 6

As Joseph's journey continues, suddenly the Cupbearer and Baker are released to attend Pharaoh's birthday celebration. Just like that, they are gone and Joseph is alone again. He asked them to remember him in their freedom – you know, put in a good word for old Joseph as this may set the stage for his release as well. But time went on and on and no update came from either one. Again, it is now Joseph and God.

Genesis 40:23 says more specifically:

"The Chief Cupbearer, however, did not remember Joseph; he forgot him."

Tracy's Prayer –

Father, I am not sure what my prayer should be right now. As I sit here and watch my mother's lifeless body being removed from the house I feel a great void in my soul. When she took her last breath it was as if a piece of me was literally torn from my body. I have prayed and prepared myself for this moment but there really is no preparation for anything like this. The mother I have known my entire life is gone. For some reason, even knowing she is with You, God, is not comforting me. Knowing I will not hear her voice again hurts beyond anything I can describe.

I feel so alone right now.

Help.

Love, Tracy

Instead of a prayer from Joseph to start this chapter, I wanted to focus on a key verse in Genesis 40 and that is verse 23, where Joseph was forgotten in prison by the only friends he had made while in custody, the Cupbearer and the

Baker. In this verse, Joseph found himself alone and abandoned – again. Now it is just him and God once again.

This chapter was probably the hardest chapter for me to write in this book. Though I have likened my walk throughout this book to Joseph's time in Egypt, this chapter captures the deepest (and darkest) emotions of my journey. When my mother passed away, I was alone in the loneliest way I had ever felt in my life. My loneliness had created an inner space in my "prison" almost like solitary confinement. I felt I only had this little window to peer out of into civilization. Death and loss have a way of doing this. They isolate you. I learned, in hindsight, this is not a safe place to be. It is definitely not safe without someone you trust near you that will not only check on you but also give you a place of accountability.

This season ended The Event and began what I will now call "The Transition"

The Transition

It is now January 2nd – the day my mother passed away. As I sit here, all my feelings of gratefulness for allowing her to make it through Christmas and the New Year's holiday seemed to have dissolved with the tears I am shedding in thinking about her no longer being in my life. With my mother's death, there is this weird, compounding emotion that I can only describe as feeling like an adult orphan because my father is also gone. I know this is not the case as I had many great years with my parents but I had this emptiness that seemed big and unfillable. It is amazing how fast things happen when a person dies – you haven't even had a chance to pull the sheets off of the bed before you are planning a funeral, looking for pictures of the family, checking your bank account to see what you can afford and, in the case of my mother's hospice care, coordinating the pickup of any equipment that may have been provided. This all occurred within the first 24 hours of my mother's passing. I, along with my brother, were busy, busy, busy during this time. No time to think about being thankful we were both there, holding her hands, as she went on to Glory in the quietness of the night. Did she hear us tell her we loved her? Did she even know we were there? I am not sure but now here we were running around trying to make sure her funeral service honored her life appropriately.

Thankfully, we were able to plan a "home-going" service for my mother in a way that truly glorified her life. From every flower to the final release of the doves – I believe she would have been proud. My hope was God allowed her to peek in and listen to some of the wonderful sentiments people said about her. Her service reiterated a saying my husband always says – that you should "give flowers to people while they are alive and can appreciate them." My Mom always worked so hard to make people feel special in their lives. I wished she could hear the fruit of her encouragement and love to those she engaged with in life. As the final attendee left and we settled into our new normal, reality began to sink in. Like Joseph, it is now You and me, God.

What was I Feeling?

To be honest, I was numb in my feelings for the first three weeks after my mother's death. I felt like most people do when they have a loved one die, especially a close relative. The grief was unbearable. I went through all the hallmarks of grief – denial, anger, bargaining – but when I hit the unexpected phase of a sadness that I would later learn was really a state of depression, it felt like I could not move from this stage. It seemed as if every disappointment or loss I'd ever experienced in my life joined forces to come and keep me company during this time. I stayed there and held on to this *depression* like a child holding their security blanket. I could not remember going through any kind of season where I felt the emotions I was feeling at that time– as an adult or growing up. I've been sad before but now it seemed like depression took this feeling to a whole new level. Depression understood what I was going through. Depression engulfed me like a big hug. It was my excuse to isolate and stay alone – to let everyone else go about their business while I tended to mine. I would say how sad I was and depression answered me with a resounding yes! It understood me. I would not want to get out of bed and it understood me so much that it allowed me to sleep for hours beyond a normal sleep cycle. No one– not my husband, friends or family understood me like depression did, though they tried. I did not want to hear from anyone in my grief. If this sounds similar to earlier chapters, it should. I felt the same feelings after *The Event* occurred but I would never have called it depression then - after all, Christians aren't supposed to get depressed right? I mean with our faith et al. we should be able to handle these emotional tailspins correct? Depression is characterized by feelings of severe despondency and dejection and yes, I believe many Christians *can* experience seasons of depression. My mother's death seemed to be the catalyst to throw me into this dark but somewhat comforting abyss. Unfortunately, in my spiritual arrogance, I felt I was resilient to this emotion after *The Event* so I did not accept this could be what I was feeling at that time. But not now. With my mother's death, I accepted it and it provided me some comfort to give my state-of-mind a name. And now, this feeling had a new, compounding emotion that I also did not know how to address - loneliness.

Lonely

Something about depression AND loneliness is deeper and scarier. If you have ever had one of those dreams where you feel like you are awake but can't move or get up, then you understand because you feel smothered. Except, I was awake but still could not move. The walls closed in and I was content to be there with no one else around. Not a healthy place to be I know, but interestingly, it was easy to get there because of the big drop in activity in my life. After all, this comes behind months of caring for my mother and the busyness of the funeral. I suddenly found myself in silence and seclusion for most of the day. This is something I had not experienced for months. I was amazed how comfortable

I felt in this solitude and found it annoying if anyone tried to come in to shake things up. This is a place I have also come to see as the door the devil uses to work his subtlest and most damaging schemes. Why? Because his number one goal is to isolate you from the things and people that can nurture and help you the most. Never mind the fact I had a caring family and village of friends that lovingly checked in on me. My rationale was I did not want to be a burden. And the Rev. Tracy part of me did not want anyone to think I could not handle what I was going through because I did not want anyone to think I doubted God. Realistically, I did not doubt God but, as I sat in my loneliness, I did wonder how God could send two powerful blows to my soul in such short order– didn't He know I was not that strong?

If Satan can get your attention focused on what you think you "don't have" vs. "what you do have" he can provide *suggestions* for you to get through what you are feeling. I admit, I was feeling open to anything that would take away the pain. My once-in-a-while glass of wine which turned into

3-4 times a week, was not covering the pain and realistically, made me feel worse. When did this habit creep in? I'm thinking somewhere around the beginning of hospice care. I began to internalize my emotions and started feeling incredibly inadequate. After all, I had lost my job and now Mom was dying. Now, after her death, I'm thinking, I did everything I could to support Mom but wondered if anything I did hastened my mother's death. Maybe I should have been more attentive or maybe more insistent she try to eat. The answer was obviously no, but when your mind is wrapped up in depression you begin to blame yourself for everything. My mind went from, *Did I mess up?* to *I am a mess up*. The devil was doing serious battle inside my head.

I felt I was broken and there was not a bandage big enough to fix this fissure in my life. The mental and emotional door had been opened and the enemy was coming in for a stay– a long stay based on the baggage he brought along.

Loneliness Leads to Brokenness

I should mention, these feelings did not take long to appear after my mother's death. I cannot even remember if I went to church during this time. I began to feel a longing to make it stop. A pill to make these empty feelings go away. I started to feel that heaven might be better than this earthly dwelling I was in– I began to contemplate taking my life. Whoa... did I just say that?! Yes, unfortunately, I did. I don't even know how serious I was, but to even have those feelings seep into my consciousness was pretty serious. I was tired of feeling tired. The grief was overbearing. I could not understand how to live life without my mother, my friend, my confidante – never mind the fact that her companionship was very limited by her fading hearing and sight and inability to remember things in recent years. Even with these infirmities, she was still a presence in my life that was now gone. I began to think about all the beautiful things I heard about heaven and they seemed better than anything I was feeling here.

I began to feel my usefulness label had expired.

You know what you do with spoiled items? You throw them away, right?

Well, not so fast. God says He does His best work with "spoiled" items. As a matter of fact, He uses old, young, big, small, rich, poor, educated, uneducated, visible, invisible, seemingly important and unimportant people all the time! He reminded me when I would try to pray that He can even use an unemployed, grieving, middle-aged, broken, lonely, depressed woman like me. Yes, even me.

What does God Say?

This chapter is significant as we will all grieve something in life. I realized that grief comes in all sizes as I felt similar feelings when *The Event* occurred. I grieved the non-existence of my job when it was gone. Though it was not to the point where I considered taking my life, these events made me realize how vulnerable we all are to sudden shifts or losses in life and how we respond to them.

While we are formulating our response to tragic events or losses in life, Satan gets busy trying to derail us so we take our focus off the promises of God - but keep in mind, God is busier. He created us and knows what we go through when life tumbles down a hill. He knows about "valley" experiences; He created valleys. He knows about our grief because He created life. That is why reading and understanding His Word, the Bible, is so important. There are lots of stories of real people losing mothers, fathers, children, spouses, jobs, status, money, reputations – you name it, it is in there – and also the redemptive work God did to comfort humanity, especially His children, in times of trouble. It is not an easy journey. If you read the story of Job in the Bible, he did not have instantaneous recovery from his troubles but he still managed to say in Job 13:15a (emphasis added): "Though he [Satan] slay me, yet will I trust in him [God]."

Job continued to trust in God even when his suffering was so painful he felt close to death.

What about Joseph?

Genesis 40:23 seems like a really sad verse. Joseph's imprisonment continued and he had the additional burden of being let down and being forgotten by his friends. The very friends that could have done something about this hell he was going through.

I should caveat again that this is my interpretation of what I think Joseph might have been feeling. We don't know if he looked at it like a hell or even perceived it as a burden. I've always wondered why these passages never elaborated on Joseph's personal feelings because it seemed he experienced disappointment after disappointment. First, he was falsely accused of a crime, then imprisoned and then forgotten. And if you go all the way back in his life, the only reason he was in this predicament in the first place was that his own brothers sold him into slavery to Potiphar.

Joseph's life seems really unfair. Do you think he thought about giving up? Do you think he considered taking his life?

We will never know but I believe the Bible intentionally leaves out some details so we can not only relate but empathize. God knows we are going to go through some Joseph-like experiences and wants us to be able to see we are not alone in what we go through. We have stories in Job's losses, Moses' insecurities, David's shortcomings and even Jesus' desertion and disappointment by some his very own disciples.

Disappointment, loss, grief, and brokenness can leave you stripped of everything that allowed you to live in the first place.

But – the Bible says – Never give up! God really does have His big, holy fingers in all aspects of our lives. He always has a plan. Everything works together for good for those that love Him and are called according to His purpose

(Romans 8:28). In fact, God has a providential, or divine, rule over all events that occur in our lives. That is His promise to us.

You may be thinking - what if I don't have the stomach (or strength) to wait this out? I know at my lowest, I could not see how I was going to last another day feeling the grief I was feeling. There was no understanding of how I was going to get from where I was to a more comfortable emotional state. Where was the map?

First, you *are* stronger than you think. I used to think I could never handle even one of the experiences discussed in this book by themselves let alone back to back, but I'm still standing.

How? We will get to that in the next chapters. In the meantime, please say to yourself out loud:

- I am stronger than I think.
- When I feel weak, I have the strength of Jesus Christ.
- Yes, I hurt but I can get up. I will get up.

- I am a fearfully and wonderfully made unique creation of God.
- God said I am beautiful and without flaw (Song of Solomon 4:7) – I *am* the beauty He made me to be!
- God has not forsaken me and knows what I am going through.

Why these declarations? Because, something about reaffirming the positive aspects of my life, especially my relationship with God, made me feel as if I was not so alone. Talking to God, as if He was a friend in the room, reminded me He hears my tears.

I said the above affirmations daily and somehow, though still sad, I was able to let a little light peek into my darkness. The light began with my daughter, Madison, who was old enough to know why I may have been feeling down, but did not understand why I was distancing myself by pushing people away.

It started one day while she was praying, when I could not find the words to pray.

I can't tell you what she said exactly, but during her prayer, her sincere words to God about being thankful for Him watching over our family- while Grandma was alive and now in her death – hit me square in the gut. Nothing had changed. I was still not working and now Mom was gone – but in her young eyes, God was still blessing us with His presence. To her, it was a time she cherished because she felt His love and the protective care of her family and village even more. This experience made her gain a greater appreciation for this little family she was a part of. And I think she understood the greater spiritual family she was a part of as well. She ended her prayer asking God to tell Grandma hello and that she missed her. With tears streaming down my face, it was the breakthrough I needed. I still had a purpose. I was not broken. My purpose was being the mother who guided her through this journey so she could also develop a faith of her own. I began to realize the true reality of what I had been contemplating in dealing with my pain. What if I had taken my life? I can't imagine the impact it would have had on her, my husband, or others. But mainly, I wondered what it would have done to my daughter's faith.

Thank you, God, for reminding me I really am stronger than I think.

Guess what – You are too!

- You are stronger than you think.
- When you feel weak, you have the strength of Jesus Christ.
- Yes, you hurt but you can get up. You will get up.
- You are a fearfully and wonderfully made unique creation of God.
- God said you are beautiful and without flaw – You *are* the beauty He made you to be!
- God has not forsaken you and knows what you are going through.

I assume Joseph said the same things when he found himself abandoned. We know he had faith in God and we know that God had favor for him. And, like some of our experiences and losses in life, none of the things Joseph experienced made any sense to him at the time. But they did not have to make sense - to him or us - as long as we remind ourselves:

- We are stronger than we think.
- When we feel weak, we have the strength of Jesus Christ.
- Yes, we hurt but we can get up. We will get up.
- We are fearfully and wonderfully made unique creations of God.
- God said we are beautiful and without flaw – We *are* the beauty He made us to be!
- God has not forsaken us and knows what we are going through.

Redeemed Reflections

What to Do When All Hope Seems Hopeless

Though the following steps are not exhaustive, it is important to recognize when you are going through a state of depression and some of the characteristics that go along with it. Remember, Christians and non-Christians are susceptible to going through depression, loneliness, and isolation when emotionally taxing events occur in life. If you find yourself going through a season of hopelessness, first recognize it is just a season and all seasons pass. Solomon prepares us for the things we WILL face in life, and their brevity, in Ecclesiastes 3. He reminds us there is a beginning and end to everything and the fact that God's promise to us is, "He is right there with us." Hebrews 13:5b says "Never will I leave you; never will I forsake you." Proverbs 12:25 says:

Anxiety in the heart of man causes depression,

But a good word makes it glad. (NKJV)

This stands as a reminder to *not be anxious for anything* (Philippians 4:6-7) but to always seek the loving and healing promises of Jesus Christ through prayer- letting Him know your feelings, requests, hopes, and desires.

The following steps are additional considerations when you are feeling hopeless:

1.Pray and give it all to God – Be Open, Be Honest, Be Raw (1 Peter 5:7). He cares for you. Remember, God is our "safe place."

Psalm 50:15 says:

And call upon me in the day of trouble: I will deliver thee, and thou shalt glorify me.

Proverbs 18:10 says:

The name of the Lord is a strong tower;

The righteous run to it and are safe.

2. Resist and recognize the beginning of isolation e.g. increased separation from people and things you once connected to. Isolation is not healthy. Find connections you trust to be accountable to. Consider counseling from a professional or clergy to provide additional guidance. Proverbs 18:1 says:

> *"A man who isolates himself seeks his own desire;*
> *He rages against all wise judgment."*

Again, broken people do broken things. Resist replace-ment behaviors that are not healthy for you – drinking alcohol, drugs (legal or not), mismanagement of money or spending, sleeping too much, etc.

James 1:12 says:

> *"Blessed is the man who remains steadfast under trial, for when he has stood the test he will receive the crown of life, which God has promised to those who love him."*

3. Resist isolating yourself from God - evidenced by not praying as much or not going to church, and continually

questioning God. Don't separate yourself from your friends or family – they love you and care for you. Ask God for wisdom to identify people you can talk to about what you are going through.

4. Recognize the ability to get through this season does not lie only with you. Seek God's love, power, and strength to forge ahead. Philippians 4:13 says:

I can do all things through Christ who strengthens me.

5. Read the stories in the Bible of other overcomers who suffered from letdowns and loss. Here are a few to consider:

- Moses - Numbers 11: 10-16
- Elijah - 1 Kings 19:1-18
- David - Psalm 51; Psalm 32
- Job – the entire book of Job is encouraging
- Jonah - Jonah 4:1-11

6. During depression and brokenness, our ability to think clearly is compromised and we do things that can damage relationships or make matters worse for ourselves. Understand that forgiveness is always available to us. Ask God for forgiveness if we do things in this season that would

disappoint Him or those close to us. He will lead you in what you need to do next. See Ephesians 1:7-9:

"In him, we have redemption through his blood, the forgiveness of sins, in accordance with the riches of God's grace that he lavished on us. With all wisdom and understanding, he made known to us the mystery of his will according to his good pleasure, which he purposed in Christ,"

The hope of our Glory is in God!

7. Find a community that specializes in working with people going through depression or needing recovery from significant life events.

One organization that helped me tremendously in my journey to recovering my life is:

<u>New Life Ministries</u>

PO Box 1029
Lake Forest CA 92609
949-494-8383

www.newlife.com

What Just Happened?

New Life offers clinical and biblical counseling resources on a number of topics that impact our lives. Their resources and nationwide counseling network gave me some perspective in understanding that my journey was not my destination and God was fully in control of leading me through and out of it.

Important: If You Are Considering Suicide – PLEASE TALK TO SOMEONE NOW!

The National Suicide Prevention Lifeline (available 24 hours/7 days a week)

1-800-273-TALK (or 1-800-273-8255) Or texting the Crisis Text Line at 741741

Their website is *http://suicidepreventionlifeline.org/*

My prayer for you:

Father in Heaven –

Please make Your presence known and visible to every soul that is reading this book. Allow them to feel your love, your care, and your direction. Make them know that whatever it is they are going through right now is not the end – but the beginning of seeing your blessings in their life. In the Bible, we read that you do your best work with the challenges we face in life. Let this season be one that not only strengthens us but transforms us from the inside out. It may be uncomfortable some days but allow your promise to NEVER leave us or forsake us make this journey one of hope as You turn this "test" into a "testimony!" Thank you for always being there, for loving us and using what we feel is broken to Your Glory!

In the mighty, healing name of Jesus Christ, I lift up this prayer,

Amen

Is That a Light?

Chapter 7

Dear God –

The warden just came in and mentioned that Pharaoh wants to see me, though he did not mention what it was about. He just told me I needed to get cleaned up. It has been two years since the Cupbearer and the Baker left and I have settled into this prison life and the daily tasks that have been assigned to me. I hope this meeting with Pharaoh is for a good reason. He has been known to murder people that he is unhappy with- at least that is what I heard about the Baker. I have fully trusted You, Lord, all through this time I have been imprisoned and I will continue to do so. I must admit, I am a bit nervous though. It has been a while since I have interacted with anyone that is not a prisoner and I don't know what is going on in the outside world. Nonetheless, whatever my fate, my hand is in Yours. One request though, please make sure I hear your voice clearly so I don't make any mistakes in the meeting with Pharaoh.

Thank you, God, for always listening.

Yours faithfully,

Joseph

It has now been 7 months since Mom has passed away. I'm starting to see a peephole of light through the crust of grief that has been over my eyes. I have had the benefit of the passage of time (I really had no choice) and some good grief counseling along the way. This has helped get me through the dark places I found myself in. My companion on the journey, depression, still tries to come in and grab me by the throat every so often but I try to keep busy to fight its presence. I have also started exercising more to lighten my mood and to regain some energy due to my lack of movement over the past year.

In this process, I've learned how the act of grieving can settle so easily into your daily routine. Though I have periods of crying my eyes out, because some innocuous thing triggers a memory of my mother, I am also going through the process of planning/thinking about what should come next.

I have felt deep in my spirit the next season God has in store for me will be unlike anything I have experienced before. I am grateful my husband allowed me to take the time I needed to get healthier emotionally and we have been able to adjust our expenses to account for the downtime. Most of my days consist of repetitive activities surrounding my daughter's schedule:

1. I get her up and ready for school.

2. I drop her off at school.

3. I come back home, do some housekeeping and look to see if there is anything I need to do to close out my mother's estate.

4. I journal my feelings for the day (God did you just tell me it's time to tell my story?)

5. I continue the work needed to set-up this new ministry about *Living the Redeemed Life,* that keeps nagging my spirit.

6. I continue the process of revising my resume and business planning to continue the job search or possibly starting a new business.

7. Uh-Oh, it is time to pick up Madison. (Where did the time go?)

8. We do homework and dinner.

9. If she does not have choir or sports practice, then it's time to get ready for bed.

10. My husband comes home, we catch up on the activities of the day.

11. Go to bed.

12. Get up and start at #1 again.

Now you might be doing the math and realize that it has been about a year since *The Event* occurred. That is about right. Though it does not have the impact on my life it used to, the lack of the daily routine the job provided is still a giant void. I am a "doer" so not "doing" what I used to do makes me feel like I am not doing enough. So, I try to keep busy doing the things I was never able to do while I was working full-time. That sounded like a riddle, didn't it?

One day, while riding home from picking my daughter up from school, something occurred that really changed my perspective on this season I was in. Madison and I had this daily routine where I would ask her about her day. We would talk about homework, life goals, friends, boys (yikes!), music; whatever she felt like discussing. As a mother, I have worked hard to make sure she knows she has an open line of communication with me so there is no topic that is off the table for discussion. We end up covering a myriad of subjects; even ones I might not be ready to discuss with a 10-year-old yet.

On this day, Madison stopped me in the middle of whatever I was yammering on about and said, "Mommy, I like this place where we are."

I responded, "Me too," thinking naively she meant she liked where we lived. (duh???)

She corrected me and said, "No, I mean this place where we can talk about different things. I look forward to this time when you pick me up. We never did this when you were working at your job."

"Really?" I responded. "We didn't talk like this when I was working at *The Event* Corporation?" (*Name changed)

"We did, but not like this, because I was always in aftercare and you were always running in at the last minute to pick me up. You would be so stressed out because you were rushing that you actually didn't speak much after we got into the car."

"Wow, Madison, I had no clue," was my response and I apologized to her if she felt slighted in any way.

In thinking about this time, she was right. My child was always one of the last ones to be picked up because I was rushing from work through the traffic and as soon as I picked her up we rushed home to cook dinner and do homework. My mind was usually distracted with whatever happened at work so I was lost in my thoughts and I would describe this behavior to her as Mommy's "decompression time." This is the life of many parents for sure, but I did not realize how disconnected I was from her feelings during that season.

Then, she said one thing that made me think deeply. She said, "Mommy, you don't have to apologize. Like I said, I like the place where we are. I would not be in the choir or be playing volleyball if we were not in *this place*."

Sadly, she was right. I never got off work in time to take her anywhere but home. In hindsight, I realize I would work until the last possible minute I could and then leave. This was always right in the middle of rush hour traffic. Thankfully, there were some activities offered as part of her aftercare but nothing like the ones she is experiencing now.

She went back to looking out the window and humming along to whatever was on the radio.

As for me, my perpetual self-loathing was stopped in its tracks and I realized I just saw a twinkling light in the dark tunnel I had allowed myself to travel in.

What was I feeling?

After we arrived home, my daughter's words just hung in my soul. I had been so focused on what I had lost in this last year that I did not step back and look at the entire picture. My loss (in my eyes) really was her gain – and mine, too. In reality, we'd had lots of surprise blessings now that we both were spending more time with each other.

An interesting shift happens when you go through a prolonged, emotionally challenging season. Your shift goes from feeling bad about the *thing* you have lost to feeling bad about *yourself* for feeling bad about losing the *thing* you lost. I know, another riddle.

It's like breaking up in a relationship, especially if it is one that you probably should not have been in any way. It is easy to get out of it, but getting over it is harder to do. First, you miss the person and you grieve. Then as time goes on you may think about what it would have been like if you had stayed with the person which makes you feel bad you are still thinking about the person. It's as if there is some timeline we all should follow to get over our feelings when challenges come and if we miss the deadline we shift the blame to ourselves. This is the self-loathing I referenced earlier because I kept berating myself for thinking about my previous vocation. I believe the cycle of always looking back creates an obstacle in our ability to heal. We need to feel what we feel, and not put ourselves down for feeling it. We should always look for the good things going on in our lives. If you take the time to look - you will find the blessings. More importantly, we should remember when Jesus walked this earth, He felt disappointment and loss just like we do. He knows what we are going through. His life reminds us that, in the blurriness of loss and challenge, we need to keep looking ahead - we *can* move forward.

Though, I had started to move past the actual occurrences of *The Event* and *The Transition*, I still dwelt in this place where I glanced back every now and then and reminisced over what I was before these events ever happened. Remembering my mother before her death was not necessarily unhealthy but replaying my last hours on the job was destroying my confidence. I continued to rehash in my head moments of my life leading *The Event* Corporation, feeling inadequate about where I was now and ultimately feeling bad about thinking these thoughts. I know some people would say, "For goodness sake, it's time to move on, Tracy" but sometimes that is easier said than done. Continuing to dwell on these memories kept me stuck and I felt a little wobbly anticipating what was to come next. I needed to find a way to get unstuck. My daughter's words were the catalyst I needed to move forward. I started to realize the healing I was seeking may very well be what I was experiencing - right now. Could it be possible it was not rolled up into a new job or new stuff to do? There are no board or staff meetings in this life and yoga pants can actually be the official uniform. Though I always considered myself a "steward" over my daughter's life, I had never really looked at the importance of what being in the moment really meant for her. Thankfully, God is always looking ahead.

What Does God Say?

When we look at the life of Joseph, I wonder if he ever felt stuck while in his predicament. Did he reminisce over his times serving Potiphar? Or even about his life with his family? It was okay to miss these things but did they make him feel better or worse?

When we are in lengthy periods of drought it can take a toll on how we view the events in our lives.

Like being in prison, it can take more than your physical body captive, it can take your thoughts captive as well.

As Joseph is requested to go and meet with Pharaoh, what do you think he was feeling? It has been years since he had experienced anything resembling 'freedom' in this ruler's kingdom and he may have lost some confidence in his ability to do what he used to do. Many times, that is why we reminisce about the good old days- because it reminds us of what we used to be.

The potential fear of failure may also have loomed heavy in Joseph's mind because, other than his service to the warden in prison, he has also been out of touch with the outside world due to his long time in prison. How are they doing things in the real world? If he failed, would Pharaoh kill him like he killed the Baker (which was what Joseph interpreted from the Baker's dream)?

What I love about the Bible is it constantly reminds us to look ahead because God is always looking to do new and different things in our lives. It emphasizes that you can remember the past but you cannot dwell on the past – even when there are great memories there! Why? Because God wants us to see what He is doing in our lives right now. Today. We can't get yesterday back and tomorrow is not guaranteed so we need to focus on where God's purpose is in our lives right now. A great quote I heard when I first went into ministry was, "God doesn't call the qualified, He qualifies those He calls." Whatever God is calling us to do, if we look to Him, we can be sure He has already mapped out the game plan. Joseph did not really have a choice to not acquiesce to Pharaoh's request without facing death. He had to face Pharaoh with an outward courage and an inward faith. We are no different than Joseph and can also do the same.

Isaiah 43:18-19 says:

> *"Do not remember the former things, Nor consider the things of old. Behold, I will do a new thing, Now it shall spring forth; Shall you not know it? I will even make a road in the wilderness and rivers in the desert.*

Staying stuck is where Satan, who is the enemy of purpose in your life, loves to keep you. Being stuck blinds you and keeps you from looking at the larger picture. Don't let him keep you there! Giving up hope for what *can* happen in the future is the one obstacle that keeps you from moving on to the next season. I also believe that expecting God to deliver you and bless you in the same ways He may have done previously has the potential to also keep you stuck because it limits what you see God doing in your life - right now. He may be taking you on a totally different journey than anything you have experienced before now!

Getting unstuck requires us to look for the points of God's light all around us. My daughter's words gave so much perspective to where I was at that time. Maybe this was really a part of God's unique plan for my life all along. Maybe this wasn't a temporary stop in the journey, but a mission aligned with a greater purpose for my life - one that was deeper than anything I was pursuing or imagined. Maybe this experience was a brick in the foundation of my daughter's purpose in life. I believe the same unimaginable purpose was in place for Joseph's life. Who knew? God knew.

Could my mother's death have been a part of the plan? I will never understand God's timing – her ultimate death was expected at some point, but it's timing at a trying time in my life – not so much. Job 14:5 says God has already numbered our days and we know we all have an appointed time to die. In this, we are reminded that our lives really are in His hands. Rather than focus on the timing of our (or our loved one's) last breath on this earth, our healing will come as we are able to look for God in the center of it all and ask Him, "What do you need me to learn from this God?" Tell Him, as I did, "My heart hurts but show me how to walk while You hold my grief. What should I be doing right now?"

God shines a light on every path you are on – even the dark ones - just look up! Even when you are on an unexpected or wrong path, if you seek Him, He will direct you to the right path (Proverbs 3:6)

Author Stormie Omartian wrote a book I read years ago entitled, "Just Enough Light for the Step I'm On." It is a great book about trusting God in the tough times. The title alone is a great example of how we should lean on God during the challenging seasons. Instead of looking at the entire staircase, let's focus on how we can be used right where God has us. Sometimes we can only see the flicker of a small light, but with God, that is all we need.

"Your word is a lamp to my feet

And a light to my path"

- Psalm 119:105

For Joseph, I imagine his release, even if it was temporary, was a light. For me, I love that God shined His light into my life on that car ride home with my daughter. Through it all, no matter how tough it has been– the memories I will leave with my daughter during this season will far outlast the memories of the job I was fired from.

"Blessed is the one who perseveres under trial because, having stood the test, that person will receive the crown of life that the Lord has promised to those who love him."

– James 1:12

Redeemed Reflections

Seeing God's Purpose in Challenging Times:

- Remember God is with you– always.
- Feel what you are feeling, but don't get stuck where you are. Determine if your thoughts are helping you or making you feel worse about your situation. Always remember, Jesus went through every emotion we experience in loss (sadness, grief, disappointment, anger, anxiousness, fear) - He understands what we are going through.
- Look around – God's blessings and beauty are everywhere in your life.
- If you can't see it – Ask God to show you His purpose for your life in this season. There really is a purpose in the pains we go through in life.

- Like a quilt square, remember this season is only one piece of the tapestry of your life.
- There is a bigger picture you are being prepared for. This season may not just be for your benefit but maybe for those around you, too!
- Be courageous as God reveals opportunities to you. Don't let fear keep you stagnant.
- Pray and meditate on God's Word every day.
- Finally, follow the Light! Many times, God doesn't give us the whole map to healing- sometimes it is just the next step.

Knowing Your Identity –
You are Reclaimed!

Chapter 8

Dear God –

First, I give all praise to You! It has been a whirlwind of activity since I was released from prison. Pharaoh has asked me to interpret some dreams that have been troubling him and keeping him up at night. To my surprise, it was the Cupbearer that suggested to Pharaoh that I be released to provide some help in understanding the meaning of these dreams. The Cupbearer?! I thought he had forgotten about me. I know that it is no surprise to You, Lord, since you direct the activities in our lives - but I'm sure you know my feelings about him and my disappointment in his silence since I have been in prison for so long.

Now the important part Lord - I told Pharaoh that it was not me that interpreted these dreams but You. I'm not scared or anything but I knew it was a risk. He had no idea of who You were but I prayed this will let him in on what I already knew – You are God. My God. You have kept me over these years and frankly I would not have survived being in prison this long without You! I have no words for my gratefulness for being one of your children. Your will be done, Lord.

Your humble servant, Joseph.

Amen

Growing up, my mother would always tell my brother and me "everyone has a story". When we would become sad because a relationship ended or we didn't get the part in a play, she would always remind us that *everyone* goes through something and we all need to find a way to get through *the moment* we find ourselves in. This was her way of letting us know we are not alone in our feelings and to remind us that eventually this too shall pass. This was the primary objective of telling my story in parallel to Joseph's - to remind you that we all have some stories to tell as the chapters are being written in our book of life. Through our eyes, the story can be tragic or a mystery or even a love story.

My assumption, if the title of this book caught your attention, is your story may include a tough challenge or a drastic change in your life. Whatever it is - because it is *your* story, God knows it is also important to you. Though the subtitle of this book is "Living the Redeemed Life When all Hell Breaks Loose," I realize that comparing our stories to 'hell' might be a bit extreme, but you know something? Our stories are *our* stories and when you are in the middle of something tough, it can feel like a nightmare that will not end.

No one can understand the underlying emotional, spiritual and sometimes physical impact of your story because they can't see inside of your mind or heart BUT the impact can sometimes feel like a literal hell. Our stories can impact us physically because of worry and anxiety. They can be more visible if we go through something like having to move out of our homes because of a divorce or lost job. It's like living in our own little isolated world where everyone goes about living their lives while we are struggling in ours.

No, they can't tell because we put our 'outside face' on to keep them from looking in, but we are hurting and need some healing. Keep in mind, everyone around us is living their stories and going through their own isolated journey, just like us, but of course we can't tell because they have their 'outside face' on too. Ironic, huh?

What Does God Say?

What are we to do as life is writing our stories, whether it be through our choices or the actions of others? How do we respond when it seems our story is taking a long time to get to the "happy ending" chapter? I'm one that sometimes rushes to the last chapter of a book to see how a story ends so it can lessen the suspense or give me some perspective on how the subject's life ends up. What happens when it seems the story continues with no happy ending in sight? I know I rely heavily on letting my faith write my story, but sometimes it feels like I am sitting on the side of life's road with a flat tire waiting for roadside service to rescue me. How do we move through the ruts we sometimes find ourselves in? More importantly, how do we live the redeemed life when there appears to be no clear path to redemption?

That is the place where we find our subject, Joseph. He is still considered a prisoner even though he has been temporarily released to interpret Pharaoh's dreams. Let's look at how Joseph responded.

After cleaning up to go meet with Pharaoh, Joseph had no control over what was going to happen next. He was still considered a prisoner and had no assurance his situation was going to change after the meeting. He had been held captive so long he really had no reason to believe his future did not include continuing to be a prisoner. More seriously– Joseph had no guarantee he even had a future because he could have been killed if he said something Pharaoh found unacceptable!

Sometimes, our stories are similar. When we are in the middle of them, we have no assurances of a happy ending. Sometimes all indications point to something not so pleasant or maybe even catastrophic. Every so often, our stories can enter a prolonged challenging season with no ending in sight. For Joseph, I imagine he was glad to enjoy the spoils of his release (e.g. a bath, food, clean clothes) but may have been wary of what was to come next. How do we, like Joseph, stay positive in the middle of *our stories* when we are not sure when our "release" will come?

Genesis 41:15-16 says:

> *Pharaoh said to Joseph, "I had a dream, and no one can interpret it. But I have heard it said of you that when you hear a dream you can interpret it."*

> *"I cannot do it," Joseph replied to Pharaoh, "but God will give Pharaoh the answer he desires."*

Let's look closely at verse 16 – Joseph tells Pharaoh out of the gate he *can't* interpret the dreams. Specifically, he says, "I cannot do it." Huh? What is he thinking? That seems to be the surest route to getting sent out to Pharaoh's gallows at worst or back to prison at best. Why would

Joseph respond so confidently with a "no" when a "yes" could have saved his life? Couldn't he at least have pretended he could do it even though God was feeding him the answers? I believe Joseph's confidence is tied to one key fact – he knew his identity. Specifically, he knew what his identity was compared to God's identity. He knew his strengths, his weaknesses, his limitations and even the fact that his ability to still be alive and to stand is tied directly to God's favor over his life. Joseph not only knew *who* he was but he also knew *Who* God was.

Verse 16 goes on and says:

> *"...but God will give Pharaoh the answer he desires."*

Joseph's faith was so strong that he knew, for sure, that God was going to tell him what Pharaoh needed to know. Joseph remembered all the times God had given him an understanding of the many wonderful dreams over his life and, even though they didn't really make sense at the time, he knew this was not a time where God was going to leave him – even if it meant facing death. His "But God" was his declaration that he knew God was with him even if it meant the potential outcome would not be so pleasant.

We need some "But God" confidence in our lives – not just when we are going through the storms of life but in everything that comes our way.

Joseph's ability to rely on God to interpret Pharaoh's dreams was not just birthed in that moment- it actually started much earlier in his life when he interpreted the dream of his sheath of wheat reigning over his brother's smaller wheat sheaths in the field (Genesis 37:5). That dream didn't make any sense then and was a contributing factor to the ongoing dislike his brothers had for him as his father's favorite child. None of that mattered because the dream was so compelling he knew he had to share it with his brothers. Then there was the Cupbearer's and Baker's dreams. Joseph could have been bitter about this gift because it hadn't particularly resulted in an ideal life for him– remember, his brothers sold him into slavery and now he was imprisoned. Joseph had to hold onto the fact that God was with him and knew what he was going through. This belief was his lifeline and God's promise to His people. By now, I suspect Joseph had come to some realization that it was no accident that he had this sensitivity to dreams, so he knew he had to rely on his faith to get him through one more- albeit a *really important* interpretation of Pharaoh's dreams.

Guess what? This is the same God who walks with us in our journeys in life – the good ones, the bad ones and even the isolated ones. We have the same promise that Joseph had because we have the same God Joseph relied on. We have even more. We have Jesus Christ and His promises in the New Testament that we are strengthened and guided by the Holy Spirit; our helper!

Redeemed Reflections

Step 1: Know Your Identity

The first step to living the redeemed life requires you to recognize your identity in God's eyes. Joseph knew his identity in God. He knew God called him by name and that he belonged to God.

We too, need to realize we are also called by name and belong to God. When you were formed in your mother's womb, God was already working out the purpose in your life. Don't let the world (or the devil) tell you otherwise. Just like Joseph, we all have a particular sensitivity to something in life – it could be art or farming, it could be accounting or helping others. It could also be something like Joseph, preaching or interpreting dreams. It is our identity and purpose that God set forth in us when we were born - set forth *specifically* for us to fulfill.

Your identity is not tied to your current circumstances— you are not a captive, a loser, too old, unequipped or (fill in the blank).

You are:

- Created uniquely by God —with a purpose and a plan

- Free – even if your current circumstances make you feel imprisoned

- An Overcomer – you *can* get through your current circumstances. Not on your strength or wisdom BUT with the loving guidance of the Holy Spirit which is the "helper" Jesus mentioned we would have to maneuver the pitfalls and opportunities of life (John 14:15-26). The Holy Spirit entered your life when you gave your life to Jesus Christ.

- Not Alone – God walks with you and has the powerful keys to deliver you from your current situation or use it to glorify His purpose (2 Chronicles 20:17).

In order to understand our identity we need to keep our focus on God– in prayer and studying the Bible. God really does speak to us through the Scriptures. I pray He is speaking to you with Joseph's story. Knowing our identity is like driving a car– to get to your destination you need to keep your eyes on the road (God). The moment you take your eyes off the road (and focus on the world), you risk getting lost or having an accident. The world will try to throw all kinds of distractions like loss, challenge, and change your way. By keeping your eyes on God, you will reach your destination or His purpose for you.

Joseph knew his identity in the Lord. Every time he prayed or relied on God he exercised this faith. When he stood before Pharaoh it was like he pulled out the equivalent of his driver's license to show Pharaoh his identity and it had on it:

> **Shepherd's License**
>
> **Name:** Joseph
>
> **Parents:**
>
>   Earthly: Rachel and Jacob
>
>   Heavenly: God
>
> **Address:** Wherever God has me

Jeremiah 1:5 tells us:

> *"Before I formed you in the womb I knew you;*
>
> *Before you were born I sanctified you;*
>
> *I ordained you a prophet to the nations."*

Though the second part of this verse was specific to the prophet Jeremiah, the first part is for all of us. God says He formed us in the womb and before we were born He gave us the gifts and authority (or identity) to walk in those gifts once we were born. We all have a purpose.

Sometimes we make intentional choices to go sideways and run away from our purpose but God says, "I'm here; look my way. Rely on me." He can lead us back if we would only look for His presence in the middle of it all.

Long before Pharaoh, Joseph knew who the keeper of his life and future was even if there was the potential for death. Joseph trusted the God he believed in.

Step 2: Know You are Redeemed

Isaiah 43:1-2 says:

> But now, thus says the Lord, who created you, O Jacob,
>
> And He who formed you, O Israel:
>
> "Fear not, for I have redeemed you;
>
> I have called you by your name;
>
> You are Mine.
>
> When you pass through the waters, I will be with you;
>
> And through the rivers, they shall not overflow you.

When you walk through the fire, you shall not be burned,

Nor shall the flame scorch you.

The Merriam-Webster dictionary defines Redeemed as *to be free from captivity by payment; to recover; to restore.* When I think of being redeemed it reminds me of the layaway process as an option to purchase clothes or products where there is a gradual payment for a lot of goods until the total price is paid in full. At that point, the items can be reclaimed from the store and are yours.

Beloved reader of this story, know that you too are redeemed! The price for you has already been paid in the death of Jesus Christ. He knew we all were facing certain death in this life because of sin and Jesus said, "I will be the payment so they can be reclaimed into the Holy family of God." God became man in Jesus (John 1:14) to suffer sure death for us! You don't have to be perfect or have your act all together to receive the love and guidance of Jesus Christ. You just need to believe in Him and recognize we are helpless without Him (John 3:16). We are sinners and need to know that Jesus is with us – in our pitfalls, prisons and isolated journeys (and everything else). He didn't promise a life of ease but, as Lord, he is offering to direct your story- if you let Him. It requires faith though, as you walk through the experience of life. Thankfully, even when we try to re-write the outcome ourselves, He is there leading us to His perfect purpose. He knows your hurts, grief, loss, anxiety, pain, lack of focus. He knows it all and, because we are redeemed, we have a caring Shepherd who is there to love us through whatever we are facing.

Jeremiah 29:11 says:

> *"For I know the plans I have for you," declares the Lord, "plans to prosper you and not to harm you, plans to give you hope and a future."*

There is a perfect plan laid out for you – whether you are still living on the fringes of this world, if you are a new believer, a "seasoned saint" or one coming back into the fold - there is a plan for your life. In the midst of hurt, loss and even potential death, that plan still prevails. That is the walk of the redeemed.

Application to My Story

As for my story, the only thing that kept me patient while my story was being re-directed and (in my mind) re-written was understanding my identity in Jesus Christ. I kept hearing this voice in my spirit say, "It is not over my child, keep going." In the middle of the night when I would cry out to God for help, I would hear, "Trust Me, you will not be overcome by this." I had to live these promises daily (sometimes hourly) just to stay encouraged. Like Joseph, I remembered what He had previously done in my life and knew He was not going to desert me now. I had to remind myself, He is a God in the valley as well as on the mountaintop - and everyplace in between. I had to resist expecting him to deliver me in ways He had done previously and, I have to admit, this part was hard to do. I would beg for God to make Himself known – right now! Many days God was silent - at least that is what I thought. It was during these times, He forced me into the Scriptures or sent an encouraging word through someone else. It seemed every sermon the Pastor preached on Sunday or I heard on the radio was just what I needed that day.

Even in His silence, God still saw me.

And even better, He heard me. I was never alone no matter how much the devil tried to convince me otherwise.

Ultimately, I learned what it meant to be redeemed. God reiterated that not only was I redeemed but He is the Redeemer and, just like Joseph, I knew I had God's favor too!

Please know and keep in the forefront of your faith - you are redeemed and have God's favor as well. That is your identity.

Postscript: God vs. Jesus vs. The Holy Spirit - What Does It All Mean?

As you are reading this story you may be asking – how do the Old Testament and New Testament books of the Bible intersect? I was always told about Jesus, but I see you referencing God throughout the book? And what about the Holy Spirit? When discussing the triune nature of God, it can get a little confusing.

Though there are many books that discuss the triune nature, or Trinity, of God, keep in mind, the story of Joseph comes long before the New Testament and the documentation of Jesus' ministry on earth. In the Old Testament, the Israelites (the chosen people in the Old Testament) only knew of God (or Lord, or Jehovah or Elohim) and were sensitive to all the laws they had been told to obey. They were promised a Mashiach (or anointed one) would come one day to rescue them in this earthly realm. As Christians, we refer to Jesus Christ as that promised Mashiach or Messiah (e.g. the Savior).

Praise God, we have the benefit of the New Testament in the documentation of the coming of the Messiah (Jesus Christ), His life, ministry and ultimately His "life-giving" death to give us all hope and a new lease on our lives. We also have the benefit of His written word, both old and new testaments, in the Bible to gain understanding of the whole story.

When I was growing up a Pastor told me, "The New Testament fulfills what the Old Testament foretells." That helped me understand the connection between the two sections of the Bible and made me understand that even with some distinct differences in these books – we need both.

To understand the nature of God, or the Trinity, my mother used to tell me that I should look at God like I look at her. She is one person but she is a mother, a sister and a daughter. One person with three distinct personalities. That helped me understand the (tri)unity of God, Jesus and the Holy Spirit at a young age and I hope this helps you too. In this book, I refer to God and Jesus interchangeably. This is the faith I know and what leads my life today.

Blessings,

Tracy

God Loves the Overcomer –
You are Restored!

Chapter 9

Dear God –

I have no words for what is happening to me right now. Well, on second thought I do have three – I Praise You!

I praise you for keeping me while I was in prison. I praise you for never leaving me and keeping me encouraged when I was discouraged. I praise you for this unusual gift you have given me to interpret dreams. I used to think it was a hindrance because the dreams many times did not make sense, but you always knew the outcome. After telling Pharaoh that his dreams meant an upcoming seven years of abundance followed by seven years of famine, I suggested to him he needed a good leader to manage these seasons. The person needed to be able to reserve and manage provisions in the high years so there would be grain and other supplies when the low years came. I really was not lobbying for the position but he offered the job to me. Me?! Joseph, the dreamer and the prisoner.

Not only did he give *me* the job, but I have new clothes – the best that you can wear in cotton and silk. He gave me jewelry; stuff I have never had. And the most precious gift? He gave me a beautiful wife! Lord, I would have been happy if he had only given me freedom from prison! Now, I have an entirely new life. I know it really wasn't from Pharaoh. He was only being used by You and I am so filled with gratitude and love that I can't keep the tears from flowing from my eyes.

I am going to do my best, Father. My best for You.

God, I am so grateful to You for everything – this is a life I could never have imagined.

Humbly and with thanksgiving,

Your servant,

Joseph.

God knows the dirt in our lives. He knows the musty, dusty, dirty paths we sometimes take to get to the next rest stop of living. Though we came into this world as clean little babies, just living and experiencing life allows things to get us dirty along the way. It can happen through our own self-inflicted acts or the actions of others. The tangible and more visible ones can seem like the giant Philistine, Goliath, that David had to fight in 1 Samuel 17. Like Goliath, they feel like a large, looming event coming straight at us, ready to consume our lives, and trying to knock us right out of our shoes.

Some events can be less visible, like when we experience a broken heart, or fear or grief. Still big, but unseen to others. They can be a health crisis that only we can see or feel but threatens to change our very existence. Even when we are fortunate enough to be on the other side of a life event, we are sometimes left with the residue of our experience to remind us of what we just came through. We are like living lint rollers picking up particles along life's way.

Our residues may manifest themselves in obvious or not so obvious ways.

Some of the things we go through leave us wondering how in the world we are ever going to feel whole again. How can we get this resulting *residue*, which feels like a stubborn stain, off of our lives? There are so many promises in the Bible of how God fights our battles but when we look at our *residue* –things aren't looking so good. The path out of this place is murky and unclear. Much like my story, if you have ever been left with unbearable grief after the death of a loved one or a diminished quality of life due to job loss or a health crisis – you may understand this statement. You could be dealing with a hairless head because of chemotherapy or an inability to do things you used to because an illness has taken your strength or a limb. Well-intentioned people around you are telling you the path to restoration is to pray more or to *hang in there*. These words are empty because the bridge to getting back what you lost was washed out in the storms of your life experience.

I imagine we sometimes feel like David in Psalm 69:17-20 when he was standing in the "residue" of his own experience -

[Lord] do not hide Your face from Your servant, For I am in trouble;

Hear me speedily.

Draw near to my soul, and redeem it; Deliver me because of my enemies.

You know my reproach, my shame, and my dishonor;

My adversaries are all before You. Reproach has broken my heart,

And I am full of heaviness;

I looked for someone to take pity, but there was none;

And for comforters, but I found none.

What are we to do when restoration is a concept not grounded in our current or future reality? Is being restored even a possibility?

What Does God Say?

Restoration is always possible; however, we may need to redefine what we think our restoration holds.

When we think about Joseph going to meet Pharaoh, we should remember he also had the "residue" of his prison experience all over him. He had no idea what was going to happen with his life and surely his best expectation was maybe Pharaoh would release him after interpreting his dreams. But would his release really be freedom? If he was not released to go back to his family, he would still be an inhabitant of Egypt and would still be bound to this kingdom as a servant, much like the Cupbearer. Would he be assigned back to Potiphar? That did not seem very appealing considering how he was treated by Potiphar's wife. What if he was sent back to prison? I imagine Joseph was feeling burdened even thinking about this option as a possibility. Why? Because if that was his best potential outcome, after meeting with the King himself, what hope would he have of ever getting out of prison in the long-term? Any of these outcomes, beyond death, were not very great options. Joseph might never have the opportunity to see his family again.

Unfortunately, when we too think of being delivered from our current circumstances, restoration can seem like an impossibility. It is during these seasons of famine and uncertainty that we can become more discouraged and frustrated. Whenever we go through the tough stuff of life, we are always thinking about what awaits us on the other side and how in the world we are going to get there. Beloved, there is something I want *you* to know - <u>don't give up hope</u>. It is during this season - of drought and uncertainty (or whatever you have named it) - that God does His best work. God loves the overcomer, especially overcomers that *overcome* because of their faith in Him.

When we think of the Israelites in the desert after being freed from slavery under *'that other'* Pharaoh (remember the 'Ten Commandments' movie – Exodus 13:17-18) we need to remember that they were first put in the wilderness *before* they were allowed entry into the Promised Land. They journeyed in the desert before they walked into the land of milk and honey. God surely could have led them directly to their new residence in Canaan, which was promised in Genesis 15:18, after they were released from bondage. Also, considering they had been in captivity in Egypt for a very, very long time (Exodus 12:40) it seemed like this should have been the next expected stop after God freed them. There were two routes to Canaan from Egypt – one was a direct route that would have taken about 4-5 days of travel and the other was one through the unfamiliar terrain of the wilderness by way of the Red Sea. Remember that miracle in the Bible (Exodus 14) where God opened up the Red Sea for them to cross through? What was God thinking when He allowed them to experience this? I believe He wanted them to have a mile marker to remember when times got tough. God gave them a miraculous experience so they would know *Who* He was. God gives us miracles every day (in the rising/setting of the sun or our heart beating in our chests) to remind us of the same.

Just like the Israelites, we too can find ourselves out in unfamiliar terrain, wandering in the wilderness with our challenging life experiences. The wilderness can be a dry and hopeless place - a place that can have us questioning God's power because we are told He has all power to change our circumstances but, for some reason, the wilderness is where we remain. There is something interesting about the wilderness though - it is in this dusty place that God redefines the "residue" of our lives. It is in the wilderness that God gives us an appreciation for His presence. It is where God takes our fears and anxieties and lets us know about His nature and the true source of our happiness. It is a place where we learn life lessons that will be needed in the future. It is also in the wilderness where we learn what faith is all about. The wilderness is where we learn to trust God.

Think of Jesus' ministry in the New Testament. He suffered the most tragic wilderness experience as He was crucified on the cross and, unlike us, Jesus *knew* this would be His outcome. Jesus also knew He needed to do this to accomplish the mission for His life - to die as a sacrifice for our sins to allow us to reach our promised land.

Jesus said in Luke 22:42, as He prayed in the Garden of Gethsemane:

> *"Father, if it is Your will, take this cup away from Me; nevertheless not My will, but Yours, be done."*

I like this verse because it shows, in Jesus' humanity, He even asked God to take away what He knew was to come. Notice that Jesus prefaced it with "if it be Your (God's) will." Substitute the word *plan* for *will* and you can understand what God is doing in your life. Jesus became an overcomer so we can overcome, but He first had to go through the *wilderness* of dying on the cross before His promised land (purpose/goal) could be entered.

Jeremiah 10:23 says:

> *I know, Lord, that our lives are not our own.*
>
> *We are not able to plan our own course. (NLT)*

We may have a plan for our lives but God's plan will always trump it. Even in our freedom to choose our path, which may include some wrong decisions, God leaves the door open for us to return to His plan. Sometimes though, to allow us to understand the journey of faith, we may need to experience the wilderness so He can teach and discipline us along the way. When God steps in and redirects us, we need to acquiesce and fall in line as He molds us for the next season.

Always remember, God wants to bless you. We are His walking, talking testimonies. As you shine, He shines but it may be through the very thing you see as a curse. God may be using what you are going through as a blessing to transform you or to touch others. Look at Joseph, his gift (that he may have seen as a curse) blessed others, even though it resulted in negative events for him. And look at God (that "But God" experience again) - when he restored Joseph it was beyond anything he could have ever expected.

Redeemed Reflections

Steps to Restoration: Repent, Reconcile, Recognize, Rejoice, and Receive

1. *Repent*

Repent, Confess, Cry Out, Go before God and ask Him for forgiveness. Leave all your concerns at His altar.

Restoration begins with us first recognizing that maybe the plans that we had or the actions we have done may have been out of alignment with His purpose for us. For example, maybe we didn't ask Him first before we entered into that relationship that ended in divorce. Maybe we did not consult him on that purchase we made or place we traveled to.

When we go through challenges, going humbly to God to ask for His mercy in our situations puts us in the posture of repentance. Ask God to reveal any areas in your life that may be keeping you in the wilderness.

Hebrews 4:14-16 says:

Seeing then that we have a great High Priest who has passed through the heavens, Jesus the Son of God, let us hold fast our confession. For we do not have a High Priest who cannot sympathize with our weaknesses, but was in all points tempted as we are, yet without sin. Let us therefore come boldly to the throne of grace, that we may obtain mercy and find grace to help in time of need."

2. Reconcile

Reconcile, or accept, your relationship with God. Stop trying to do *life* all by yourself. You are not alone. He is called *Father* for a reason – He loves you and will watch over you and protect you as you grow in faith. Joseph never lost his faith in God, even during challenging times. We should do the same.

John 15:4 says:

> *"Abide in Me, and I in you. As the branch cannot bear fruit of itself, unless it abides in the vine, neither can you, unless you abide in Me."*

3. Recognize

Recognize who your real source of strength (and life) is - Jesus Christ. Always remember the love of Jesus never fails. If something is blessed by Jesus Christ it is still blessed by Him, even if it gets broken, lost, hurt or off-track.

The Blood of Jesus Christ never takes a break in our lives. His mission on the cross still lives actively in our lives – whether we are in or outside the wilderness.

Philippians 4:19 says:

> *"And my God shall supply all your needs according to His riches in glory by Christ Jesus."*

4. Rejoice

Praise God always. Praise chases the enemy away. Praise strengthens your heart and faith. Praise paves the way for restoration.

Rejoice in the fact that God has given you another day to make a difference.

Psalm 118:24 says:

> "This is the day the Lord has made;
>
> We will rejoice and be glad in it."

Rejoice in the fact that Jesus has already overcome whatever the world tries to throw at you. All you need to do is stand on your faith in Jesus Christ, even if it is as small as a mustard seed, when *wilderness life* comes your way - He will get you though.

1 John 5:4 says:

> "For whatever is born of God overcomes the world. And this is the victory that has overcome the world—our faith."

5. Receive

Receive what God has for you. Remember, God is Sovereign. He has dominion over all things and is omniscient (e.g. knows everything that is going on).

Psalm 103:19 says:

> "The Lord has established His throne in the heavens, And His sovereignty rules over all."

Providence is the means by which God directs all things; both seen and unseen, good and evil, toward a worthy purpose. God is providential. He is never out of control. Just like Joseph, things may happen to you that, however unpleasant, can have a purpose and plan to work out positively because you love Him. You don't need a contingency plan – trusting God is the <u>only</u> plan you need.

Romans 8:28 says:

> "We know that in all things God works for the good of those who love him, who have been called according to his purpose."

Understand, like Joseph, your blessing may not come when you want it and it may not come in the package you are expecting.

God is not recycling you (e.g. reusing an old version of you) or your blessings – He is building something new!

Application to My Story

What I have learned in this journey is restoration is a process, not an event. As I sought the Lord to understand what my next season would be, I had to first resist the temptation to re-create what I had already done in my previous season. I confess, I tried to rebuild a replica of what I had lost. I actually created another company and tried very hard to make it similar to the one I was previously with. All the while, God kept telling me "Not now" and was pressing me hard to put pen to paper and document the lessons learned in this journey. I questioned whether this was His voice or mine, constantly wondering why in the world God would want me to do this. Was this the best use of my time?

Interestingly, it was my husband who continued to encourage me to share my testimony. He kept telling me, "Write your story, it might help someone." I did not take into account the fact he was also praying to God for direction for me, and for us because his life had changed too with these events. Because I never imagined myself as an author, let alone doing ministry in any full-time capacity. In fact, this was the furthest thought from my mind. Ultimately, this was where I was being led so I had to *Receive* it (see Step 5 above). When God has a plan for you, He will use the people around you to ensure you get the message. Be careful though - stay *prayed up* - because the enemy will try to do the same if he suspects God has any plans for your life. Like my depiction of Joseph, I had to overcome my fears and reservations. I still am working through them but with a focus of increased faith and discernment. It took me a while to realize my previous journey, in many ways, had prepared me for this next season – however different it was shaping up to be!

We have to resist the temptation to look at God as the Bam! miracle worker (think of the Chef, Emeril Lagasse's signature move). Please know, God *is* capable of doing the instantaneous, Red Sea miracles in our lives but, the real lesson of faith and perseverance is generally found in the journey through the wilderness. That is where we learn the true character and love of God.

Remember, God loves the Overcomer. Remember, God loves you.

Ephesians 3:20 says:

Now to Him who is able to do exceedingly abundantly above all that we ask or think, according to the power that works in us, to Him be glory in the church by Christ Jesus to all generations, forever and ever. Amen.

When the Lord restores you, it is beyond anything we can imagine. Put your imagination down and let Him fulfill your dreams.

You are Rejoiced!

Chapter 10

Joseph is blessed beyond anything he could have expected.

Joseph is loved beyond anything he can fathom.

You are too.

You are Rejoiced!

This final chapter is different from previous chapters. While there is no prayer from Joseph to begin the chapter, if I had to come up with one it would have been filled with nothing but praise and hallelujahs for the Lord. From Genesis 41 through 50, we see testimony after testimony of how God can take a seemingly fretful situation and turn it into a blessing. Not only was Joseph's life blessed, but those that were associated with him were blessed too. God's favor was demonstrated visibly to those around him in the new position he now held as Pharaoh's Second-in-Command as Egypt prospered during the seven years of abundance that had been predicted. And, in the "imagine this" category - Joseph was now even Potiphar's boss! The blessings continued during the subsequent seven years of famine and this is where we pick up the story. The main objective of this chapter (and living the redeemed life) is remembering one important thing: You are so loved by our Heavenly Father that He can take the deepest of valley situations and make them blessings. The book of Genesis, and really the entire Bible, is God's love letter to us all. Why? Because God loves you, always.

Now, let's look at the life of our protagonist, Joseph, in the final chapters of Genesis.

Joseph has now actively assumed his new role as the Chief Administrator for Pharaoh and is busily preparing Egypt for the predicted years of abundance and famine. Joseph's story could have stopped right there and this would have been considered a happy ending. It is always nice to see a story, especially true stories, end on a positive note.

Thankfully, when we work in the realm of an omnipotent and all-knowing God, He always likes to remind us there is more to the story and that is where we pick up Joseph's life.

Joseph was 30 years old when he stood before Pharaoh after being released from prison.

Joseph went to work promptly planning the infrastructure and processes needed to store up and meter out resources during the seven years of abundance. Pharaoh gave Joseph full authority to put in place whatever was needed to be successful and God used Joseph mightily during this time. God blessed Joseph professionally and personally as well - through the birth of two children which he named Manasseh and Ephraim. Though we don't see many descriptors of what Joseph felt during most of his captivity in Egypt or even in his release, the meanings of his son's names give us a glimpse into Joseph's inner feelings and faith during this time. In Genesis 41:51-52 we see –

Joseph called the name of the firstborn Manasseh: "For God has made me forget all my toil and all my father's house." And the name of the second he called Ephraim: "For God has caused me to be fruitful in the land of my affliction."

Look closely at verse 51 and the meaning of the name of Joseph's firstborn son, Manasseh - "God has made me forget all my toil and my father's house." This thought could be seen as a positive or a negative. Joseph recognizes God's involvement in allowing him to forget his past accomplishments, to include his family and home life. Depending on your perspective, this could be viewed as a negative because Joseph might be angry with God if those memories have faded so much that he is frustrated because he can't remember the minute details of his upbringing. Or, and I believe this to be the case, Joseph could be thanking God that the memories of his past life and the family he may never see again are not so prominent that they torture him day in and day out. He did not say the memory was wiped out – no one can forget the *existence* of some people and events – but the impact of their loss is not as strong as it used to be. Said another way, going back to the example of a relationship that ends or even the grief of losing a loved one - the passage of time *and* God's cover can allow you to move on in life and eventually, however painful the event was, the sting of it will fade to a tolerable and sometimes non-existent level. In my own life, though I still grieve the loss of my mother (and father) and have days where I miss her terribly, the impact is not as haunting as it was in the six months after her death and I do feel a little better each day. I believe though, you need God's presence in the center of your life to allow this to resolve positively to ward off bitterness and allow forgiveness.

Looking at the meaning of his second son's name, Ephraim, we are reminded that God *is* present in our afflictions – our wilderness situations – and can use you and bless you through them. Joseph recognized that Egypt had been the home of his long imprisonment and some unpleasant memories, but God was also planting good memories to replace or overcome the ones he would probably like to forget. Even though Joseph was still in Egypt, God was still blessing him. This was not just for Joseph – God is present in your "Egypt situations" as well and He wants you to be fruitful and blessed even while you are traversing the wilderness to your healing.

In Genesis 42, we see some significant events occur:

- After the seven years of abundance ended, the seven years of famine began.
- Because of Joseph's wisdom, grain had been stored up for this season. The inhabitants of Egypt (and beyond) now had a source for food as the famine consumed their ability to grow new crops.
- The news that Egypt had available grain reached Joseph's father and brothers in Canaan who, out of necessity, traveled to Egypt to purchase food
- It is here that Joseph is reunited with his brothers.

But, as I said earlier, God says "there is always more to the story…"

When Joseph's brothers arrived in Egypt he recognized them but, possibly due to the passing of time and the natural aging process, they did not recognize him. For some reason, Joseph chose to keep his identity a secret as he arranged a reunion with his father, Jacob, and his younger brother Benjamin. They both had not traveled to Egypt with the other brothers. Though Joseph caused the brothers some grief for a few days before he sent them back to Canaan (he accused them of being spies and imprisoned them) he still sent them home with food and supplies. This interaction with them caused Joseph to be overwhelmed with emotion (Genesis 42:24) and he privately cried.

This scene reminds me of what our heavenly Father must think when He is loving us through our ups and downs. Joseph held his brothers in captivity for a few days before allowing them to go back home. Though the Scripture does not go into detail on why he felt the urge to do this, the brothers thankfully remembered and recognized what they had done to their younger brother (Joseph) back when they sold him into slavery. The brothers took the time to repent before God. As we traverse through our ups and downs in life, we too need to pause and take the time to apologize for our sins, especially in the areas where we were culpable in the sin. Once released, Joseph sent his brothers home with an abundance of grain and provisions though he kept one of the brothers (Simeon) in Egypt to force a return visit in which the brothers would bring back his younger brother, Benjamin, who he had really missed over these years. Joseph's response to his brothers reminds us that God walks with us even when we don't understand what in the world He is doing. Joseph blessed his brothers despite the fact they were the reason he was in Egypt in the first place. God, amid His desire to bless us, also recognizes that love – true love – requires the ability to look beyond our faults and the faults of others. We are His children and because of that, God always sees the best in us – even through the fog and grime that life leaves on our souls.

The brothers arrive home but the food eventually runs out and the brothers need to return to Egypt to purchase more grain. To the consternation of Jacob, they need to bring Benjamin along because that was Joseph's demand if they were to return to Egypt. Looking at this through the eyes of Jacob, he must be feeling very distraught because he has now lost two sons - remember, Joseph kept his brother Simeon behind in Egypt (Genesis 42:24) and Jacob was not privy to the whole story of Joseph's captivity. Joseph was considered dead from his perspective since that was what his sons told him about his disappearance. Jacob had no desire to send his youngest son, Benjamin, to Egypt and potentially lose three sons. I imagine Jacob was going through his own wilderness journey as a result of these events. I am compacting many of the events and dialogue of these chapters into an abbreviated overview so please take some time later to sit back and read Genesis 42-44 quietly. There is a lot of richness in the story of Joseph and his brothers and their journey to forgiveness.

In Genesis 44, the brothers return to Egypt, with Benjamin in tow and, to their surprise, they are greeted on their arrival by Joseph with food and fellowship. As if this event is not confusing enough (remember, they still don't know he is their brother Joseph) we read that again, Joseph falsely accuses the brothers of stealing from him. Specifically, it is Benjamin, the youngest, he accuses and threatens to put Benjamin in prison.

What are we to make of this? Wasn't Joseph held in prison for many years due to a false accusation? Considering what he had been through, why would he put his brothers through this? In this passage, we can't really discern if he was trying to get revenge on his brothers for what they had done to him BUT what we can see is the ultimate result – *everyone involved had a change of heart.*

That is the point here. In life, we will go through some challenging experiences. Some confusing, baffling events that make us question if God really hears us or even knows us. Well, there is one thing we can know for sure –

God does hear you and knows you – He made you. He loves you so much that He sometimes allows you to go through the unpredictable bends of life to mold your hearts (and faith) in a way that you truly can feel His presence and know His love. In this world where good and evil co-exist, the closer you get to God's love, the more the devil is going to vex and try to distract you. That is not always a bad thing; it means you are growing closer to God and His purpose for your life.

To complete this story, when Joseph sees the anxiety of his brothers after accusing them falsely of stealing he can't keep his identity hidden anymore and eventually tells them who he is. Though they felt ashamed of what they had done to Joseph so many years ago, they also realized the providential love of God. What does that mean? It means God's hand is in everything – whether we are the source or the involuntary victims of our challenging circumstances. In this meeting of Joseph with his brothers, we see both sides of the coin on how events occur in our lives and how God moves in the background to bring them to a resolution aligned with His purpose. Sometimes the resolution may be painful and not be what we wanted but it will be resolved - whether it be here on earth or in the spiritual realm after death - it will be resolved. We have seen the involuntary wilderness that Joseph experienced just because he was doing his job for Potiphar *and* we have also seen how God used his experience to elevate him to a place of blessing and authority.

God still blessed and provided for Joseph's brothers, in spite of their actions in contributing to Joseph's initial imprisonment. Only God could have written a story where their lives would intersect in the most unexpected circumstances and still be blessed – in the middle of a famine!

Joseph put it all together in the words he said to his brothers when he revealed his identity. In Genesis 45:4-8 we read:

And Joseph said to his brothers, "Please come near to me." So they came near. Then he said, "I am Joseph your brother, whom you sold into Egypt. But now, do not therefore be grieved or angry with yourselves because you sold me here; for God sent me before you to preserve life. For these two years the famine has been in the land, and there are still five years in which there will be neither plowing nor harvesting.

And God sent me before you to preserve a posterity for you in the earth, and to save your lives by a great deliverance. So now it was not you who sent me here, but God; and He has made me a father to Pharaoh, and lord of all his house, and a ruler throughout all the land of Egypt.

Huh? Whoa. Did Joseph just imply that maybe he went through all of this to quite possibly glorify God? That God knew this famine was coming and He needed someone like Joseph in place to "preserve lives by a great deliverance?" Well...yes he did. In verse 8, he states "God sent me here. Not you." We too, can't predict the route God takes us on but we can be confident that He controls the map, the navigation, the geography, the topography, the weather and the people along the way. That is the promise we have as we put our trust in Him - even when the unthinkable and unpredictable happens. Why? Because you are cherished; you are rejoiced! Even if the result of what we experience is death, our reward is not on this earth (Matthew 5:11-12). It is in heaven with Jesus if we have accepted Him as our Savior.

Remember: there is nothing we can do to separate ourselves from God's love. Nothing. Nada. Even when we try to run away from Him, God loves us. God loves us beyond anything we can imagine – nothing gets in the way of God's pursuit of us. Why? Because He loves us.

Romans 8:37-39 says:

"Yet in all these things we are more than conquerors through Him who loved us. For I am persuaded that neither

death nor life, nor angels nor principalities nor powers, nor things present nor things to come, nor height nor depth, nor any other created thing, shall be able to separate us from the love of God which is in Christ Jesus our Lord."

As believers, who have accepted Jesus Christ as our Savior, we can never "sin away" our salvation. If we have not yet accepted Him as our Savior we can never "sin away" our opportunity for salvation. This is important because the devil sometimes uses guilt and hard times to keep us from having a relationship with Jesus. Romans 8 reminds us that God always has the door open to be in a relationship with Him and to experience His love. I am reminded of this when I think of the two prisoners next to Jesus on the cross. He offered relationship (salvation) to both, but only one accepted. As death was imminent, one of the prisoners recognized he did not have a chance to "get it right" before he died and Jesus Christ offered him salvation right there. Jesus promised him a place in heaven just because he believed (Luke 23:39-43).

As the story of Joseph comes to a close in Genesis 50 we see the true power of forgiveness and a great example of how our trials can be turned into blessings that can touch lives beyond our own. Joseph is eventually reunited with Jacob and the entire family was allowed to live and prosper in Egypt. Joseph's brothers and their families were even elevated to a place of blessing just because they were associated with Joseph! This would never have happened if Joseph did not go through the trials he experienced.

In the close of this chapter, Joseph speaks to his brothers to let them know:

"But as for you, you meant evil against me; but God meant it for good, in order to bring it about as it is this day, to save many people alive." (Genesis 50:20)

God has a way of turning our *hellish* or "what just happened" situations into the platform for our blessings and future successes. Why? Because He loves you and wants the best for you as His child. Jesus Christ says He came for us to have *"life more abundantly"* (John 10:10). Keep your eyes open - because your *abundance* may come dressed in something far different than what you expect and the route it takes to get to you may be bumpy. With God though, the journey will be worth it and paved with His love. Let God love you today. You are Rejoiced.

Redeemed Reflections

Understanding God's Love for You:

- God can bless you (and even those connected to you) because of your faithfulness.

- During times of famine (emotional, physical, spiritual, mental), God is ever-present. Joseph not only blessed his family, but as the famine worsened, Joseph's wisdom allowed others all over the land to use Egypt's resources to provide for their families (Genesis 47).

- Sometimes, God does His most visible work during our seasons of famine. Be obedient to His Word and listen to His Voice.

- There is a purpose for your life. God loves you so much that He can use your pain to help others and yourself. Your faithful purpose glorifies Him.

- Song of Solomon 4:7 says *"You are all fair, my love, and there is no spot in you."* God is always looking beyond what we see in ourselves as issues - He sees perfection.

- Romans 5:8 says *"But God shows his love for us in that while we were still sinners, Christ died for us."* In our imperfection, Jesus Christ loved us enough to die for us.

- Isaiah 43:4-5 says *"Since you were precious in My sight, You have been honored, and I have loved you; Therefore I will give men for you, And people for your life. 5 Fear not, for I am with you; I will bring your descendants from the east, and gather you from the west"*. We can walk courageously because God is with us.

- John 3:16 says *"For God so loved the world that He gave His only begotten Son, that whoever believes in Him should not perish but have everlasting life."* God loved you enough that He gave His life to give you eternal life. You have a hope beyond these earthly experiences.

- Jeremiah 31:3 says *"The Lord has appeared of old to me, saying: "Yes, I have loved you with an everlasting love; Therefore, with lovingkindness, I have drawn you."* You were created in love and with love, uniquely, by God Himself.

- Ephesians 2:10 says " *For we are His workmanship, created in Christ Jesus for good works, which God prepared beforehand that we should walk in them.*" You were created to do good works. There is purpose *in* you!

This is just a handful of what the Bible says about God's love and hope for us. The entire Bible is God's love letter to us to let us know just how rejoiced we are to Him.

Afterword

During the season in which this book was written, I literally saw every priority in my life get turned upside down. Prior to *The Event* if you asked me to describe myself I would have introduced myself as Tracy Graves Stevens, CEO of *The Event* Corporation with many years of experience in blah, blah and more blah, blah, blah. I would eventually get to the ordained minister part and then mention my family. These were the roles I played but none of the items in my previous description inherently spoke to *who* I really was and my real identity. Now- if you ask me who I am, I say – Tracy Graves Stevens. Survivor. Seeker. Beloved of God - Redeemed, Restored and Rejoiced. Also, Madison's Mom and Garry's Wife (these roles are the inherent ones that God wants to be priorities after Him). I have found that people are far more interested in this part of me than the other things I used to say.

My story is still being written. I have had the opportunity to see my now middle-school daughter thrive in sports and academics. She is growing into this phenomenal young lady that sincerely loves the Lord. My husband and I have grown deeper in our walk with Christ (and each other - even after 22 years together). We have adjusted to a new way of life and have resumed the date-nights we had lost to my continual pattern of working late. I also learned to shift my prayers from, *God, restore what I lost in this season* to *Bless my husband as the head of our family - restore us in Your Will through him.* My goodness - it has been amazing to see how God has blessed him in his faith walk, his job, and ultimately our family. Like Joseph's brothers, I guess this trial was as much for him as much as it was for me.

Not long ago, I heard a sermon by Rick Warren, the Pastor of Saddleback Church, where he said, *"God will sometimes take your income, influence, and identity to humble you so He can use you."* I fully understand this statement, as I lost these very things so God could redefine my life to His purpose for it. Those things of the past were only there for a season and I now see God was readying me for a new season. I do have times when I fight with the memories of what I used to do and where God is trying to take me. Sometimes, those old fears and insecurities rear their heads in my life and I have to press into Jesus to keep them at bay. Realistically, I never would have dreamed that I would one day publish the book you are reading. This is a story born from the journey. If the journey did not occur, I may not have experienced the deeper discernment I now have in my relationship with God. Every single day I ask the Lord, *What do you want me to do?* and I am learning constantly to wait for His answer. I am also learning to *receive* it as well. I admit, there are days when I glance back and wonder what it would have been like if *The Event* had not occurred BUT God's loving care through this journey has only given me the assurance that I am exactly where He wants me to be. I really am purposefully planted. I realize more now than ever, through the trials and celebrations that life brings my way - that I am Reclaimed. I am Restored. I am Rejoiced.

I am Redeemed.

You are, too.

That is what *Living the Redeemed Life* is all about my friends. Embrace it.

"But now, thus says the Lord, who created you, O Jacob,

And He who formed you, O Israel:

"Fear not, for I have redeemed you;

I have called you by your name;

You are Mine.

When you pass through the waters, I will be with you;

And through the rivers, they shall not overflow you.

When you walk through the fire, you shall not be burned,

Nor shall the flame scorch you."

Isaiah 43:1-2

"Now may our Lord Jesus Christ Himself, and our God and Father, who has loved us and given us everlasting

consolation and good hope by grace, comfort your hearts and establish you in every good word and work."

2 Thessalonians 2:16-17

Scriptures References Supporting the Prayers of Joseph

- *All References are from the New King James Translation (NKJV). Public domain.*
- *Scripture quotations marked (NLT) are taken from the Holy Bible, New Living Translation. @1996, 2004,2007,2013, by Tyndale House Publishers, Inc., Carol Stream, Illinois 60188. All Rights Reserved.*

Introduction: Genesis 39:1-19

Chapter 1: Genesis 37:36 and Genesis 39:20-23

Chapter 2: Genesis 39:20-40:4

*Key verses Genesis 39:21, 40:4

Chapter 3: Genesis 40:1-4

Chapter 4: Genesis 37:5-28 and Genesis 40:5-8

Chapter 5: Genesis: 40:9-23

Chapter 6: Genesis 40:23

Chapter 7: Genesis 41:9-14

Chapter 8: Genesis 41:15-16

Chapter 9: Genesis 41:17-41

Chapter 10: Genesis 41-50

Acknowledgements

So many people that encouraged me along the way (please forgive me if I miss anyone's name). I live by the Scripture, "Nothing is impossible with God" (Luke 1:37), but when it came to authoring a book, I felt that was an area that was <u>not</u> possible. I thank the many encouraging souls that told me, "Yes, you can and we can't wait."

For God - the Father, the Son, and the Holy Spirit. The Book you hold is the direct inspiration from my Lord and Savior, Jesus Christ. I want to thank God for using me, a leaky pot, for His will. I'm sorry I ran from You for so long and I am so grateful You continued to pursue me. You knew better.

For my beloved husband, Garry – the one I call my "human tissue." You caught my tears and listened to my frustrations as I doubted everything about my life when my purpose was revised. You encouraged me even as I questioned if I really had a story to tell. I thank you for your support and your care for our family during the ups and downs. You truly are a man of God and the one my soul loves.

For my daughter, Madison – Girl, you know Mommy loves you so much! You have listened to me go on and on about different aspects of this book and prayed with me when the attacks would come to stifle my faith – we covered a lot on those car rides across Maryland! You truly are a gift and I thank God He trusted me and Daddy to be your stewards here on earth. You have a purpose, my lady – live your life redeemed!

For My Village – Gary Graves, Pastor Linda Stevens, Angela Proctor Brown, Dr. Renette Dallas, Revs. Joy and David Douglas, Pastor David Watts and Rev. Robyn Watts – You all have lived this journey with me and prayed with me along the way. Thank you for being that "rest in green pastures" (Psalm 23:2) when I needed it most. I love you all.

For My Cheerleaders– My Aunties – Bonita Bond, June Mullins, Dorothy Freeman; Allyson Hall Spivey, my former co-workers, Leesa and Shannon Arnold, Pastor Henry Davis and my First Baptist Church of Highland Park family, the Graves/Martin/Saunders/Robertson clan, my extended family (every one of you) – I say, thank you.

For My Prayer Circle – God's Prayer Warriors - Michelle Bell Smith, Sharon Harris, Janet Miller. Every week, twice a week for over the past decade we have come together, trusting God in prayer. We have seen Him move miraculously! Your faith is amazing. I am so grateful for you all. Let God continue to use you in this wonderful way.

For Michelle Jones   All I can say is "you are power." I am in awe of your undying faith in God and how you have stepped out and taken this faith nationwide. I thank you for re-igniting a fire within me as the enemy has worked hard to extinguish it.

For 'The C12 Group' (Christian CEO Peer Advisory Team) – Ken Gosnell and the Rockville, MD Chapter – my advisors, peers, and friends in this journey of business leadership. I am grateful for your advice and encouragement when the "high times" shifted and I was left trying to figure out *what just happened.* Your counsel has gotten me ready for whatever God has next.

For the Starbucks Crew in Calverton, Maryland and Silver Spring, Maryland (Bel Pre Road location) - Day after day I would come in and write. I loved the white noise (and coffee) the atmosphere provided. Your congeniality, support, and fellowship encouraged me daily. You probably don't realize how much you touch the lives of the people that come through your stores. I want to thank you for touching mine in a such a positive way.

For Amy Brooks, CEO of VoicePenPurpose – Your diligence in pulling my story out and pushing me along is truly appreciated and I give you a resounding "thanks." You have a gift and a destiny. Continue to let God use you in "helping others to help others" in telling their stories as well.

For Eddie Egesi – Your talent is inspiring, and your persistence is appreciated. As we went back and forth over the designs for this book, you guided me along when I did not have a clue. You have a great future ahead of you. Thank you for letting me be one of the stepping stones along the way.

And last, but not least, Mom and Dad (Mary and Bernard Graves) - You two worked hard to instill so much in me to build a legacy for generations to come. I pray, as you look down from Heaven on my life, that I have made you proud. I love you.

-Three Generations -

Me, my Mom, and Madison

About the Author

Tracy Graves Stevens, an ordained minister for over 15 years, lives by the Scripture that there is nothing impossible with God. A seasoned corporate leader, Graves Stevens is the Founder of Redeemed Life, LLC which focuses on ministering through the broken times of life and Trusted Beacon, LLC, a professional services firm. She is a wife, mother, speaker, team builder and encourager. Graves Stevens resides with her family in Silver Spring, Maryland.

Visit her website at **www.TracyGravesStevens.com**

www.ingramcontent.com/pod-product-compliance
Lightning Source LLC
Chambersburg PA
CBHW051751040426
42446CB00007B/311